Internet of Things P with ESP32

Build exciting and powerful IoT projects using the all-new
Espressif ESP32

Agus Kurniawan

BIRMINGHAM - MUMBAI

Internet of Things Projects with ESP32

Commissioning Editor: Vijin Boricha
Acquisition Editor: Prachi Bisht
Content Development Editor: Aishwarya Moray
Technical Editor: Prashant Chaudhari
Copy Editor: Safis Editing
Language Support Editor: Storm Mann
Project Coordinator: Nusaiba Ansari
Proofreader: Safis Editing
Indexer: Priyanka Dhadke
Graphics: Tom Scaria
Production Coordinator: Arvindkumar Gupta

First published: March 2019

Production reference: 1290319

Published by Packt Publishing Ltd.
Livery Place
35 Livery Street
Birmingham
B3 2PB, UK.

ISBN 978-1-78995-687-0

www.packtpub.com

`mapt.io`

Mapt is an online digital library that gives you full access to over 5,000 books and videos, as well as industry leading tools to help you plan your personal development and advance your career. For more information, please visit our website.

Why subscribe?

- Spend less time learning and more time coding with practical eBooks and Videos from over 4,000 industry professionals

- Improve your learning with Skill Plans built especially for you

- Get a free eBook or video every month

- Mapt is fully searchable

- Copy and paste, print, and bookmark content

Packt.com

Did you know that Packt offers eBook versions of every book published, with PDF and ePub files available? You can upgrade to the eBook version at `www.packt.com` and as a print book customer, you are entitled to a discount on the eBook copy. Get in touch with us at `customercare@packtpub.com` for more details.

At `www.packt.com`, you can also read a collection of free technical articles, sign up for a range of free newsletters, and receive exclusive discounts and offers on Packt books and eBooks.

Contributors

About the author

Agus Kurniawan is an independent technology consultant, author, and lecturer. He has over 18 years' experience working on various software development projects, including delivering training courses and workshops, and delivering technical writing. He has done a few research activities related to wireless networking, software, and security in multiple universities. Currently, he is pursuing a Ph.D. program in Computer Science in Germany. He has previously written five books for Packt.

About the reviewer

Catalin Batrinu is an Electronics, Telecommunications and Information Technology graduate from the Politehnica University of Bucharest. After 5 years in applications development, where he helped companies move applications to the cloud, he moved to IoT. He has prototyped irrigation controllers, smart sockets, window shutters, lighting controls, environment controls et cetera, all controlled over the cloud. As an IoT Architect, he develops augmented/virtual reality frameworks, sensors and digital twin concepts, corresponding software architecture related to Big Data, real time performance, and structured/unstructured data analysis and modelling. He also identifies data sources, defines the single point of truth, and ensures data security.

Packt is searching for authors like you

If you're interested in becoming an author for Packt, please visit `authors.packtpub.com` and apply today. We have worked with thousands of developers and tech professionals, just like you, to help them share their insight with the global tech community. You can make a general application, apply for a specific hot topic that we are recruiting an author for, or submit your own idea.

Table of Contents

Preface

ESP32 is a low-cost MCU with integrated Wi-Fi and BLE. Various modules and development boards-based ESP32 are available to build **Internet-of-Things (IoT)** applications easily. Wi-Fi and BLE are common network stacks in IoT applications. These network modules can fulfil your business and project needs, providing cost-effective benefits.

This book will serve as a fundamental guide to developing an ESP32 program. We will start with GPIO programming, which will involve some sensor devices. Then, we will get deep into ESP32 development by building some IoT projects such as a weather station, a sensor logger, a smart home device, a Wi-Fi camera, and Wi-Fi Wardriving. Lastly, we will enable ESP32 to interact with mobile applications and cloud servers such as Amazon AWS.

By the end of this book, you will be up and running with various IoT projects based on the ESP32 chip.

Who this book is for

This book is designed for students, professional designers, developers, and IoT enthusiasts. Basic knowledge of ESP32 is not required to work with the content of this book.

What this book covers

Chapter 1, *Getting Started with ESP32*, presents a review of the ESP32 board. We also set up a development environment for ESP32 boards.

Chapter 2, *Making Visual Data and Animation on an LCD*, offers a brief introduction to weather systems. Here, we'll make a simple ESP32 program to sense temperature and humidity using the DHT22 sensor module. Furthermore, we'll work with the LCD on the ESP32 board, accessing the LCD modules through the ESP32 board.

Chapter 3, *Building a Simple Game with an Embedded ESP32 Board*, teaches you how to work with an analog joystick, along with an exploration of a simple sound device with a sound buzzer, and the development of a simple game.

Chapter 4, *Building a Sensor Monitoring Logger,* covers how to work with external storage, such as SD cards and microSD cards, on an ESP32 board. We'll store our sensor data on external storage, and use a sensor monitoring logger by applying sleep mode after sensing and storing sensor data.

Chapter 5, *Controlling IoT Devices over the Internet,* covers how to work with Wi-Fi on an ESP32 board. Our ESP32 board will be connected to the internet and accessed over a web server. We'll also make a simple web server inside the ESP32 board. Lastly, we'll build a simple smart home device by controlling an LED over a network.

Chapter 6, *Building an IoT Weather Station,* takes the reader through building a weather station with ESP32 and DHT22. We'll also extend our weather station with Node.js in order to serve massive requests.

Chapter 7, *Making Your Own Wi-Fi Wardriving,* teaches the reader how to access the GPS module on the ESP32 board. We'll build a simple wardriving project to perform Wi-Fi profiling on a GPS location. We'll see how to read Wi-Fi SSIDs and GPS data simultaneously.

Chapter 8, *Building Your Own Wi-Fi Cam,* outlines how to work with the camera module on the ESP32 board. Here, we'll use the OV7670 camera module to capture images. We'll also develop Wi-Fi functionality to take a picture over a network.

Chapter 9, *Making IoT Devices Interact with Mobile Applications,* outlines how to develop an ESP32 program and an Android application, and then make the two interact using the Wi-Fi protocol as a communication medium. You can use this approach to control some sensor and actuator devices on the ESP32 board via an Android application. We'll learn how to build a BLE service on the ESP32 board, and cover how to make interactions between the ESP32 board and mobile Android through BLE.

Chapter 10, *Building IoT Monitoring with Cloud Technology,* covers operations in AWS IoT. We'll create an ESP32 program to send temperature and humidity sensor data to AWS IoT, and build a communication link between AWS IoT and ESP32 over MQTT. This skill can be extended to other IoT devices.

To get the most out of this book

This book is intended for anyone who wants to learn IoT development with ESP32. The following is a list of required skills for this book:

- You should have basic knowledge of the C or C++ programming languages.
- Having basic knowledge of IoT concepts will help the reader when following the exercises in this book, but isn't necessary.

Download the example code files

You can download the example code files for this book from your account at `www.packt.com`. If you purchased this book elsewhere, you can visit `www.packt.com/support` and register to have the files emailed directly to you.

You can download the code files by following these steps:

1. Log in or register at `www.packt.com`.
2. Select the **SUPPORT** tab.
3. Click on **Code Downloads & Errata**.
4. Enter the name of the book in the **Search** box and follow the onscreen instructions.

Once the file is downloaded, please make sure that you unzip or extract the folder using the latest version of:

- WinRAR/7-Zip for Windows
- Zipeg/iZip/UnRarX for Mac
- 7-Zip/PeaZip for Linux

The code bundle for the book is also hosted on GitHub at `https://github.com/PacktPublishing/Internet-of-Things-Projects-with-ESP32`. In case there's an update to the code, it will be updated on the existing GitHub repository.

We also have other code bundles from our rich catalog of books and videos available at `https://github.com/PacktPublishing/`. Check them out!

Conventions used

There are a number of text conventions used throughout this book.

`CodeInText`: Indicates code words in text, database table names, folder names, filenames, file extensions, pathnames, dummy URLs, user input, and Twitter handles. Here is an example: "Mount the downloaded `WebStorm-10*.dmg` disk image file as another disk in your system."

A block of code is set as follows:

```
int16_t temperature = 0;
    int16_t humidity = 0;
    if (dht_read_data(sensor_type, dht_gpio, &humidity, &temperature)
== ESP_OK){
```

When we wish to draw your attention to a particular part of a code block, the relevant lines or items are set in bold:

```
int16_t temperature = 0;
    int16_t humidity = 0;
    if (dht_read_data(sensor_type, dht_gpio, &humidity, &temperature)
== ESP_OK){
```

Any command-line input or output is written as follows:

```
$ make menuconfig
```

Bold: Indicates a new term, an important word, or words that you see onscreen. For example, words in menus or dialog boxes appear in the text like this. Here is an example: "Select **System info** from the **Administration** panel."

Warnings or important notes appear like this.

Tips and tricks appear like this.

Get in touch

Feedback from our readers is always welcome.

General feedback: If you have questions about any aspect of this book, mention the book title in the subject of your message and email us at customercare@packtpub.com.

Errata: Although we have taken every care to ensure the accuracy of our content, mistakes do happen. If you have found a mistake in this book, we would be grateful if you would report this to us. Please visit www.packt.com/submit-errata, selecting your book, clicking on the Errata Submission Form link, and entering the details.

Piracy: If you come across any illegal copies of our works in any form on the Internet, we would be grateful if you would provide us with the location address or website name. Please contact us at copyright@packt.com with a link to the material.

If you are interested in becoming an author: If there is a topic that you have expertise in and you are interested in either writing or contributing to a book, please visit authors.packtpub.com.

Reviews

Please leave a review. Once you have read and used this book, why not leave a review on the site that you purchased it from? Potential readers can then see and use your unbiased opinion to make purchase decisions, we at Packt can understand what you think about our products, and our authors can see your feedback on their book. Thank you!

For more information about Packt, please visit packt.com.

Getting Started with ESP32 1

ESP32 is a low-cost chip that consists of MCU with Wi-Fi and a Bluetooth network stack that makes it possible to build an **Internet of Things** (**IoT**) application. In this chapter, we will review ESP32 boards and learn ESP32 basic development.

We will also cover the following topics:

- Introduction to ESP32
- Reviewing development boards-based ESP32
- Setting up a development environment
- Building ESP32 programs with Espressif SDK
- Developing Sketch programs on ESP32 development boards

Technical requirements

Before we begin, make sure you have the following things ready:

- A computer with an OS installed such as Windows, Linux, or macOS.
- An ESP32 development board. Recommended is the ESP-WROVER-KIT v4 board from Espressif.

Introduction to ESP32

ESP32 is a low-cost Wi-Fi and Bluetooth chip from Espressif Systems. ESP32 integrates Wi-Fi (2.4 GHz band) and Bluetooth 4.2 solutions on a single chip. It also supports classic Bluetooth for legacy connections such as L2CAP, SDP, GAP, SMP, AVDTP, AVCTP, A2DP (SNK), and AVRCP (CT). ESP32 also supports **Bluetooth Low Energy** (**BLE**), which covers L2CAP, GAP, GATT, SMP, and GATT-based profiles. A detailed product review of the ESP32 chip/module can be found at the following link: `https://www.espressif.com/en/products/hardware/esp32/`.

There are two forms for ESP32: chip form and module form. ESP32 chip and module forms have different sizes and numbers of pins. Choosing ESP32 form is dependent on your design and purposes. The size factor of ESP32 form can also be one of your preferences when you make and design an IoT solution-included PCB scheme. A list of ESP32 chips and modules can be read on the following website: `https://www.espressif.com/en/products/hardware/modules`.

Next, we will review some development boards that use the ESP32 chip or ESP32 module.

Reviewing development boards-based ESP32

Since ESP32 has two forms, in chip and module, there are some development boards with an ESP32 chip or ESP32 module. In this book, we will not learn how to make a board-based ESP32. Instead, we will use pre-existing, ready development boards available on the market.

We can categorize boards-based ESP32 into two models. The first board models are the development boards officially manufactured by Espressif. The second models are from their partners or personal makers.

Let's review some available ESP32 development boards on the market.

The official ESP32 development kit

In general, Espressif provides an ESP32 development kit board that we can use directly. We don't need to take any effort to make a PCB board and do soldering of the ESP32 chip. A list of ESP32 boards from Espressif can be found at this link: `https://www.espressif.com/en/products/hardware/development-boards`. We will review the two ESP32 boards: ESP32-PICO-KIT and ESP-WROVER-KIT boards.

ESP32-PICO-KIT is a basic development board that is small in size. This board fits on breadboard PCB, so you can do wiring on it. The board consists of EPS32 chips such as serial USB CP2102 (version 4.0)/CP2102N (version 4.1). You can connect this board to a computer through USB.

ESP-WROVER-KIT is a complete development board. This consists of various sensors and modules. The board uses ESP32-WROVER for ESP32 board implementation. The following are the main features from ESP-WROVER-KIT:

- JTAG interface on FT2232HL
- Camera connector
- I/O connector
- RGB LED
- Micro SD card slot
- LCD

A form of ESP-WROVER-KIT can be seen in this photo:

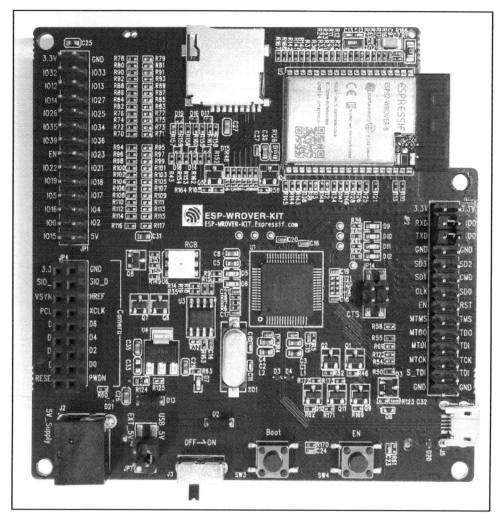

ESP-WROVER-KIT

Third-party boards-based ESP32

We can buy ESP32 chips and modules from Espressif and their distributors. Then, we can make our own development board for ESP32. Sometimes, these boards-based ESP32 boards are sold to the public. In this section, we will review two ESP32 development boards.

SparkFun ESP32 Thing is one of the ESP32 development boards from SparkFun. This board uses the ESP32 chip. The board provides TTL USB to make it possible to communicate with the ESP32 chip. In addition, *SparkFun ESP32 Thing* has an LiPo connector so we can run the board with a battery. For further information about SparkFun ESP32 Thing, you can visit on this site: `https://www.sparkfun.com/products/13907`. A form of the SparkFun ESP32 Thing board is shown in the following photo:

SparkFun ESP32 Thing

Adafruit is an electronic manufacturer and electronic product online store. They make a development board-based ESP32 called Adafruit HUZZAH32 – ESP32 Feather Board. This board uses the ESP32 module. Adafruit HUZZAH32 has a TTL USB and LiPo connector like the SparkFun ESP32 Thing board. You can visit `https://www.adafruit.com/product/3405` to purchase this board:

Adafruit HUZZAH32 – ESP32 Feather Board

Other board-based ESP32 boards can be found on Alibaba and AliExpress. You can search for `ESP32 board` as keywords. There are many custom development boards with ESP32 chips or modules.

In this book, I use ESP-WROVER-KIT for testing.

Setting up the development environment

Espressif provides SDK development for ESP32. Technically, there is a guideline document from Espressif on how to set up the ESP32 toolchain. You can follow this guideline for Windows, Linux, and macOS: `https://docs.espressif.com/projects/esp-idf/en/` `latest/get-started/index.html#setup-toolchain`.

After completed, you can continue to get ESP-IDF to enable you to develop the ESP32 program. You also need all required libraries for Python. A detailed guideline can be read on this site: `https://docs.espressif.com/projects/esp-idf/en/latest/get-started/` `index.html#get-started-get-esp-idf`.

If done, we can develop programs for the ESP32 board. The ESP32 program is written in C programming language, which you should be familiar with. However, we can write ESP32 programs using any text editor. In this book, I use Visual Studio code: `https://code.` `visualstudio.com`. This IDE tool is available for Windows, Linux, and macOS.

Next, we develop a simple program with the ESP32 board.

Demo 1 – building your first ESP32 program

In this section, we will write a simple program for the ESP32 board. We need three LEDs including cable jumpers for this. We will turn on one LED from LED 1 to LED 3. For implementation, I use the ESP-WROVER-KIT board.

Let's begin.

Wiring

We connect three LEDs on the ESP32 board GPIO. We then do the following wiring:

- LED 1 is connected to IO12
- LED 1 is connected to IO14
- LED 1 is connected to IO26
- All LED GND pins are connected to the ESP32 board GND

You can see a wiring scheme in the following diagram:

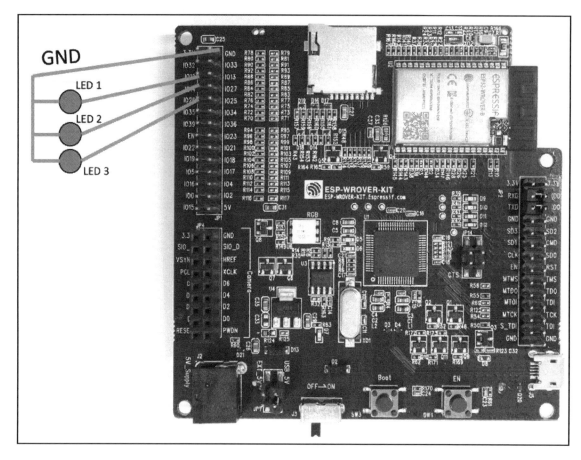

Wiring on LED demo

Next, we create a project.

Creating a project

In general, there is no project template for the ESP32 program with SDK. However, we can create a project with the project structure as shown in this screenshot:

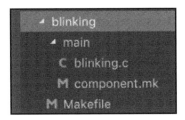

A project structure

Each project has the following files:

- `Makefile` on your project root
- `main` folder
- Program file (`*.c`)
- `component.mk` file inside the `main` folder

In this demo, we create a project by creating a folder called `blinking`. Then, we create a `Makefile` file. We also create a `main` folder. Inside the `main` folder, we create the `blinking.c` and `component.mk` files.

We will write code for those files in the next section.

Writing the program

Now, we write scripts and codes on the `Makefile`, `component.mk`, and `blinking.c` files:

1. In the `Makefile` file, we declare our project name. This should be the same name as the project folder. The following are `Makefile` scripts:

```
PROJECT_NAME := blinking

include $(IDF_PATH)/make/project.mk
```

2. `component.mk` is required for compiling purposes. You should create a component file with this exact name. The content of the `component.mk` file is empty:

```
#
# "main" pseudo-component makefile.
#
# (Uses default behavior of compiling all source files in
directory, adding 'include' to include path.)
```

3. Now, we write code for our main program, `blinking.c`. Firstly, we declare our required library headers as follows:

```
#include <stdio.h>
#include "freertos/FreeRTOS.h"
#include "freertos/task.h"
#include "driver/gpio.h"
#include "sdkconfig.h"
```

4. We define our three LEDs on ESP32 GPIO. We use IO12, IO14, and IO26 pins from ESP32 GPIO:

```
#define LED1 12
#define LED2 14
#define LED3 26
```

5. A main entry of the program is `app_main()`. For this, we create a task and pass a function, called `blinking_task`:

```
void app_main()
{
    xTaskCreate(&blinking_task, "blinking_task",
configMINIMAL_STACK_SIZE, NULL, 5, NULL);
}
```

6. The `blinking_task()` function performs GPIO initialization by calling `gpio_pad_select_gpio()`. Then, we set the GPIO pin as output using the `gpio_set_direction()` function. In the main loop, we turn on the LEDs one by one. We call the `turn_on_led()` function to perform this task:

```
void blinking_task(void *pvParameter)
{
    // set gpio and its direction
    gpio_pad_select_gpio(LED1);
    gpio_set_direction(LED1, GPIO_MODE_OUTPUT);
    gpio_pad_select_gpio(LED2);
    gpio_set_direction(LED2, GPIO_MODE_OUTPUT);
```

```
gpio_pad_select_gpio(LED3);
gpio_set_direction(LED3, GPIO_MODE_OUTPUT);

int current_led = 1;
while(1) {
    turn_on_led(current_led);
    vTaskDelay(1000 / portTICK_PERIOD_MS);
    current_led++;
    if(current_led>3)
        current_led = 1;
}
}
```

7. To turn on/off LEDs, we call `gpio_set_level()` with 1 or 0 parameters. If we pass 1 on `gpio_set_level()`, it means we set a power voltage on that GPIO:

```
void turn_on_led(int led)
{
    // turn off all leds
    gpio_set_level(LED1, 0);
    gpio_set_level(LED2, 0);
    gpio_set_level(LED3, 0);

    switch(led)
    {
        case 1:
            gpio_set_level(LED1, 1);
            break;
        case 2:
            gpio_set_level(LED2, 1);
            break;
        case 3:
            gpio_set_level(LED3, 1);
            break;
    }
}
```

8. Now, save all programs.

Next, we configure the project before flashing on the ESP32 board.

Configuring the project

Now, we should configure our project using `menuconfig`. This tool is a part of the ESP32 toolchain that you have configured previously on your platform.

Open Terminal and navigate to your project directory. Then, you can type this command:

```
$ make menuconfig
```

You should get the dialog shown in the following screenshot:

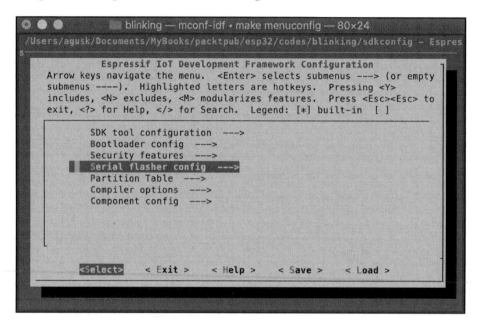

Espressif project config

We configure our ESP32 serial port and then select the `Serial flasher config` menu. From here, fill your serial port of the ESP32 board. You can see my ESP32 serial port from the ESP-WROVER-KIT board here:

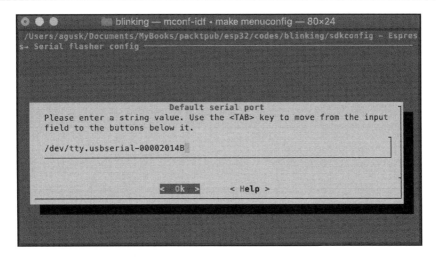

Setting a serial port for the ESP32 board

If complete, click the **Save** button. The menuconfig program will save your project configuration. The program output can be seen in the following screenshot. You should see that this tool generates the sdkconfig file into your current project directory:

```
/esp/esp-idf/tools/kconfig/lxdialog/yesno.c -o lxdialog/yesno.o
cc -c -D_DARWIN_C_SOURCE -I/opt/local/include -DCURSES_LOC="<ncurses.h>" -DNCUR
SES_WIDECHAR=1 -DKBUILD_NO_NLS -Wno-format-security -DLOCALE -MMD /Users/agusk
/esp/esp-idf/tools/kconfig/lxdialog/menubox.c -o lxdialog/menubox.o
cc -o mconf-idf mconf.o zconf.tab.o lxdialog/checklist.o lxdialog/util.o lxdialo
g/inputbox.o lxdialog/textbox.o lxdialog/yesno.o lxdialog/menubox.o -lncurses -L
/opt/local/lib -lncurses
cc -c -D_DARWIN_C_SOURCE -I/opt/local/include -DCURSES_LOC="<ncurses.h>" -DNCUR
SES_WIDECHAR=1 -DKBUILD_NO_NLS -Wno-format-security -DLOCALE -MMD /Users/agusk
/esp/esp-idf/tools/kconfig/conf.c -o conf.o
cc -o conf-idf conf.o zconf.tab.o -lncurses -L/opt/local/lib -lncurses
DEFCONFIG
#
# configuration written to /Users/agusk/Documents/MyBooks/packtpub/esp32/codes/b
linking/sdkconfig
#
MENUCONFIG


*** End of the configuration.
*** Execute 'make' to start the build or try 'make help'.

GENCONFIG
agusk$
```

A result of configuring a project

Now, your program is ready for compiling and flashing.

Compiling and flashing

After we configured our project, we can flash our program into the ESP32 board. We can type this command on the current project directory from the following terminal:

```
$ make flash
```

This command performs compiling and flashing. If the make command is not found, you should install make for your platform.

If you have configured a serial port of the ESP32 board, the program will be flashed. Otherwise, you will get a timeout because the tool cannot find the ESP32 serial port. You can see my program output on the flashing process in the following screenshot:

```
● ● ●                    blinking — -bash — 80×24
None
MAC: 30:ae:a4:ef:4b:e8
Uploading stub...
Running stub...
Stub running...
Configuring flash size...
Auto-detected Flash size: 4MB
Flash params set to 0x0220
Compressed 22992 bytes to 13646...
Wrote 22992 bytes (13646 compressed) at 0x00001000 in 1.2 seconds (effective 151
.3 kbit/s)...
Hash of data verified.
Compressed 155488 bytes to 74039...
Wrote 155488 bytes (74039 compressed) at 0x00010000 in 6.6 seconds (effective 18
8.7 kbit/s)...
Hash of data verified.
Compressed 3072 bytes to 103...
Wrote 3072 bytes (103 compressed) at 0x00008000 in 0.0 seconds (effective 1534.4
 kbit/s)...
Hash of data verified.

Leaving...
Hard resetting via RTS pin...
agusk$
```

Flashing a program into the ESP32 board

If this succeeds, you should see lighting on LED 1, LED2, and LED 3.

Next, we develop the ESP32 program using Arduino Sketch.

Arduino programming for ESP32

Arduino is the biggest community for open source hardware. It has various Arduino boards to fit your needs. Arduino also provides software to develop the Arduino program, Sketch. Arduino Sketch can be downloaded at `https://www.arduino.cc/en/Main/Software`.

Now, ESP32 boards support Arduino development. Technically, ESP32 development with Arduino still uses Espressif SDK. You should set Arduino Sketch software to enable you to work with ESP32 boards. You can configure this based on your platform. Please follow this guideline on the following website: `https://github.com/espressif/arduino-esp32`.

It is recommended to install ESP32 boards into Arduino software via Board Manager. Open the **Preferences** dialog from Arduino, then put this URL into the board manager URL: `https://dl.espressif.com/dl/package_esp32_index.json`:

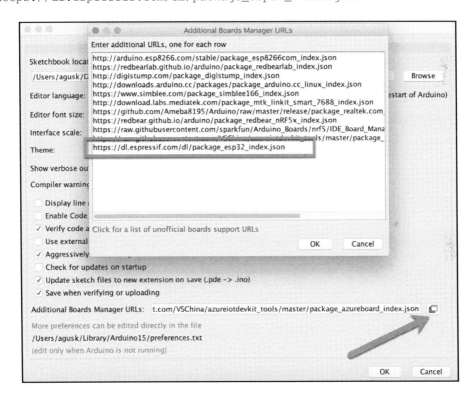

Adding ESP32 boards into Arduino software

When this is done, click OK.

Now, you can install ESP32 boards. To do this, open **Boards Manager** from the **Tools** menu. Type esp32 on this form so you can see the esp32 package, as shown in the following screenshot:

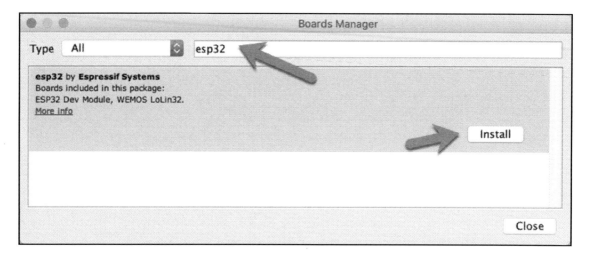

Installing ESP32 boards

After you have clicked **Install**, Arduino will download all required libraries for ESP32. If done, we will see a list of ESP32 boards on the Arduino software. You can see this in the following screenshot:

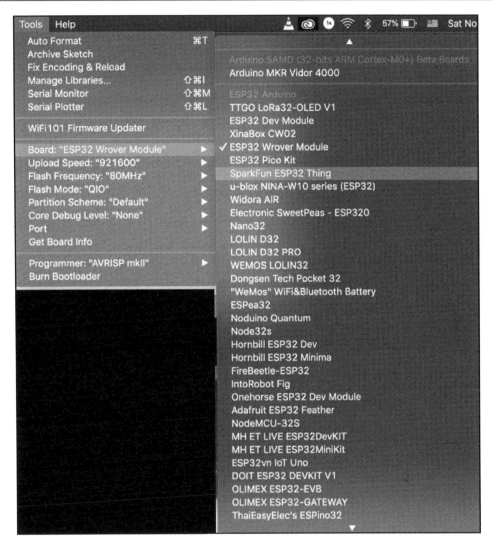

A list of ESP32 boards in Arduino

Now, your Arduino is ready for ESP32 boards.

Demo 2 - making an Arduino Sketch program with ESP32

In this section, we develop an Arduino program for ESP32 boards. We will use the previous demo, but we still use Arduino software. If you don't have experience with Arduino Sketch, I recommend learning Sketch programming on this site: `https://www.arduino.cc/reference/en/`. Since ESP32 has two cores (core 0 and core 1), our Arduino program runs one core. You don't need to worry which about core will be used by Arduino. You can verify which core is used with the `xPortGetCoreID()` function.

1. We use the `pinMode()` function to set ESP32 GPIO pins as input or output. Then, we can write digital values using the `digitalWrite()` function. Using the previous demo, we can implement the demo using Sketch, as follows:

    ```
    #define LED1 12
    #define LED2 14
    #define LED3 26
    ```

2. Let's set the `current_let` to 1. That meant that later will start turning the LEDs with LED number 1.

    ```
    int current_led = 1;
    ```

3. Every program developed with the help of Arduino IDE will contain the `setup()` function. Code in setup function will run only on time at the beginning. For now let's setup the pins that will drives our LEDS as output pins.

    ```
    void setup() {
      pinMode(LED1, OUTPUT);
      pinMode(LED2, OUTPUT);
      pinMode(LED3, OUTPUT);

    }
    ```

4. This is a helper function that will get a led number as parameter and will turn off all the LEDS and based on the value of the input parameter will turn on that LED by using the `digitalWrite()` function.

    ```
    void turn_on_led(int led)
    {
      // turn off all leds
      digitalWrite(LED1, LOW);
      digitalWrite(LED2, LOW);
      digitalWrite(LED3, LOW);
    ```

```
switch(led)
{
case 1:
digitalWrite(LED1, HIGH);
break;
case 2:
digitalWrite(LED2, HIGH);
break;
case 3:
digitalWrite(LED3, HIGH);
break;
}
}
```

5. The code in the `loop()` function will run continuously like in a `while(1)`. For now the code will turn on one LED every second. When the code reach the last LED then will go back to the first one and the process will run forever.

```
void loop() {
turn_on_led(current_led);
delay(1000);
current_led++;
if(current_led>3)
current_led = 1;
}
```

6. Save the program.

Now, you can set the ESP32 board target and its port, as shown in the following screenshot:

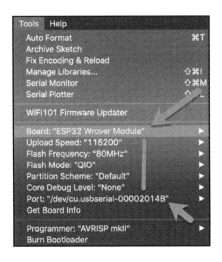

Configuring the ESP32 Wrover module

Now, you can compile and upload the Sketch program via Arduino software. If you succeed, you can see the program output as shown in the following screenshot:

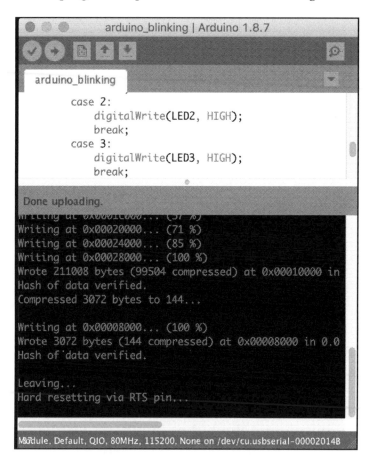

Uploading the Sketch program to the ESP32 board

If you still get errors, please verify your ESP32 board type and its serial port.

Summary

In this chapter, we have learned about and reviewed the ESP32 board. We have also set up a development environment for ESP32 boards. At the end of the chapter, we developed a blinking program for three LEDs using Espressif SDK. Lastly, we implemented the same scenario using Arduino software.

In the next chapter, we will learn how to work with LCDs on the ESP32 board.

Further reading

For more information on ESP-IDF programming, I recommend reading: the ESP-IDF Programming Guide, at https://docs.espressif.com/projects/esp-idf/en/latest/.

2
Making Visual Data and Animation on an LCD

The ESP32 chip and module consists of **general-purpose input/output (GPIO)** pins to enable sensing and actuating. In this chapter, we will learn how to read sensor data from the ESP32 GPIO. We will also talk about using an LCD to display data with the ESP32 chip. In addition to this, we will show sensory information such as temperature and humidity in the LCD. Ultimately, we will build a simple IoT weather monitoring system with the ESP32 board.

We will see how to work with an LCD by following step-by-step instructions. You will also learn how to use the ESP32 board to detect the weather and display it on LCD by the end of this chapter.

The following topics will be covered in this chapter:

- Introduction to ESP32 GPIO
- Introduction to IoT for weather monitoring systems
- Reading temperature and humidity from a sensor device
- Displaying information using an LCD
- Making a weather monitoring system

Technical requirements

Before we begin, make sure that you have the following things ready:

- A computer with an OS, such as Windows, Linux, or Mac, installed.
- An ESP32 development board. The ESP-WROVER-KIT board from Espressif is recommended.
- An ESP32 development environment configured on your computer.

- An DHT22 sensor module.
- The CoolTerm tool, which can read and write data over serial communication (UART). This is available for Windows, Linux, and Mac. We set our serial tool to the ESP32 board with Baudrate 115200.

Introduction to ESP32 GPIO

The ESP32 chip features forty physical GPIO pads. Some GPIO pads cannot be used or do not have the corresponding pin on the chip package. For development boards based on the ESP32 chip or module, some board makers probably expose all ESP32 GPIO pins. However, some board makers also expose ESP32 GPIO pins but add additional pins such as battery, voltage, exclusive sensor, and ground.

Since there are many ESP32 development board models, we cannot explore all board models. Instead, we will focus on the ESP-WROVER-KIT board from Espressif.

We can access GPIO pins on the ESP-WROVER-KIT board with three locations. You can see these locations from the ESP-WROVER-KIT board in the following image. Some GPIO labels are shown in the board body so that we can see all of the GPIO pins:

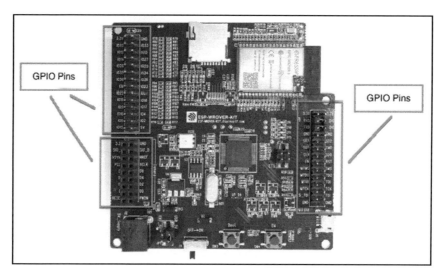

Figure 2-1: GPIO pins from an ESP-WROVER-KIT board

Some GPIO pins are used for PWM, ADC, DAC, I2C, I2S, and SPI. You can find this GPIO layout from the ESP-WROVER-KIT board in the following document: `https://dl.` `espressif.com/dl/schematics/ESP-WROVER-KIT_V4_1.pdf.`

Now that we've picked a board on which to work, let's get a brief overview of IoT for weather monitoring systems before we begin setting one up.

Introduction to IoT for weather monitoring systems

A weather monitoring system senses the state of the atmosphere, such as its temperature, humidity, and weather conditions (clear, stormy, and so on). To get the state of the atmosphere, we need sensors.

We can design a simple model for an IoT weather monitoring system as shown next in Figure 2-2. An IoT board with sensor devices can sense physical conditions such as temperature and humidity. Some IoT weather monitoring systems can display their sensor values on a monitor or LCD display:

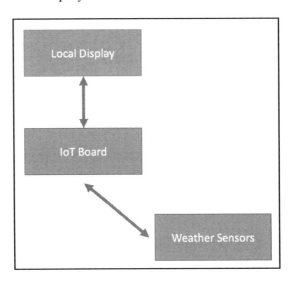

Figure 2-2: A simple model for an IoT weather Monitoring System

Now that we've discussed the weather monitoring system and its basic architecture, let's start building our weather monitoring system. In the next section, we'll learn how to read temperature and humidity using a sensor device and an ESP32 board.

Reading temperature and humidity from a sensor device

In this section, we'll build a simple program to read temperature and humidity from sensor devices. We'll use the DHT22 sensor module for this. This sensor device is easy to find on online stores such as Adafruit, SparkFun, and AliExpress.

Our project scenario is to read temperature and humidity values from a sensor device. Then, we will print sensor values on a serial Terminal. After doing this, we will implement our hardware wiring and develop a program.

Wiring

Let's begin by exploring the DHT22 sensor module. This module can sense temperature and humidity. In general, the DHT22 has four pins. You can see the sensor pinout in Figure 2-3:

Figure 2-3: A general pinout for a DHT22 sensor module

For our demo, we need to wire the hardware as follows:

- Connect DHT22 pin 1 to the ESP32 board 3.3V.
- Connect DHT22 pin 2 to the ESP32 board GPIO 26 (IO26). You can add a pull resistor 4K7 (optional).
- Connect DHT22 pin 4 to the ESP32 board GND. You can add a pull resistor 4K7 (optional).

You can see my hardware wiring with the ESP-WROVER-KIT board and DHT22 in Figure 2-4:

Figure 2-4: A wiring sample from my hardware

Now that we have covered hardware wiring, let's move on to writing the program.

Building a program

Building a program for ESP32 is a multi-step process. Let's look at each step and begin our build for the weather monitoring system:

1. Create a project called `dhtdemo`. Please read `Chapter 1`, *Getting Started with ESP32*, which describes how to create an X project. Our main program is the `dhtdemo.c` file.

2. To access the DHT22 sensor, we can use the DHT library from the ESP-IDF component libraries: `https://github.com/UncleRus/esp-idf-lib`. This project consists of some drivers for sensor and actuator devices that are compatible with the ESP32 chip/board. You can use these drivers for your own projects. In this section, we use the `dht` driver to enable working with the DHT sensor device.

3. Copy the `dht` components folder from the `esp-idf-lib` project into your local `esp-idf/components` folder. You can see that my `dht` component has been copied in Figure 2-5:

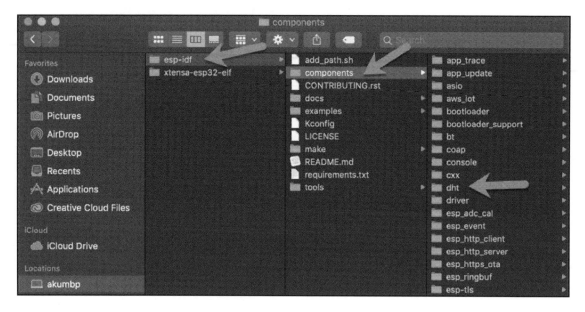

Figure 2-5: Adding the dht component on ESP-IDF

4. Now, we will write our program on the `dhtdemo.c` file. Firstly, we define our required libraries for our ESP32 board. The header files that will be loaded in our program are as follows:

```
#include <stdio.h>
#include "freertos/FreeRTOS.h"
#include "freertos/task.h"
#include "driver/gpio.h"
#include "sdkconfig.h"
```

5. We declare the `dht.h` header to access the DHT library. We also define our DHT model as `DHT_TYPE_DHT22`. Lastly, we set GPIO 26 for the DHT22 sensor module:

```
#include <dht.h>
static const dht_sensor_type_t sensor_type = DHT_TYPE_DHT22;
static const gpio_num_t dht_gpio = 26;
```

6. Now, we will write the main entry program, `app_main()`. We create a task by calling the `dht_task()` function. Then, we call the `dht_task()` function using `xTaskCreate()`:

```
void app_main()
{
    xTaskCreate(&dht_task, "dht_task", configMINIMAL_STACK_SIZE, NULL, 5,
NULL);
}
```

In the `dht_task()` function, we read the temperature and humidity from DHT22 using the `dht_read_data()` function. The results of the reading sensor are stored in two variables: temperature and humidity. These sensor values will then be printed on the Terminal using `printf()`.

This program will read sensor data every five seconds. You can write this complete program for the `dht_task()` function as follows:

```
void dht_task(void *pvParameter)
{
    int16_t temperature = 0;
    int16_t humidity = 0;
    while(1) {
        if (dht_read_data(sensor_type, dht_gpio, &humidity, &temperature)
== ESP_OK)
            printf("Humidity: %d%% Temp: %d^C\n", humidity / 10,
temperature / 10);
        else
            printf("Could not read data from sensor\n");

        vTaskDelay(5000 / portTICK_PERIOD_MS);
    }
}
```

Save all codes in the `dhtdemo.c` file and then compile and flash to the ESP32 board.

Running the program

Now, you can configure your project with the `make menuconfig` command. You can carry out this task with the blinking project that we looked at in Chapter 1, *Getting Started with ESP32*.

After our program is flashed into the ESP32 board, we can use a serial program such as PuTTY or CoolTerm. For the demo, I used CoolTerm. You can download this tool from the following link: `http://freeware.the-meiers.org`.

You can then open a connection to the ESP32 board. If this is successful, you will see our program output on a serial tool. You can see my program output in Figure 2-6:

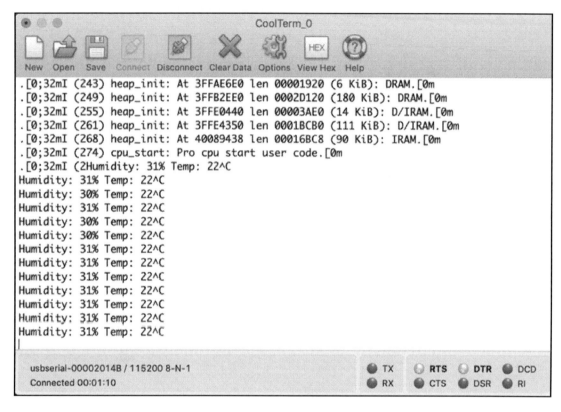

Figure 2-6: Program output on the CoolTerm serial app

Now that we've configured our sensors to read temperature and humidity, let's look at displaying this information using an LCD.

Displaying information using an LCD

In this section, we will work with an LCD on ESP32 boards. This demo uses the ESP-WROVER-KIT v4 board, which has a built-in ILI9341 model LCD. You can read an ILI9341 LCD datasheet at the following link: `https://cdn-shop.adafruit.com/datasheets/ILI9341.pdf`.

For implementation, we will use the TFT library for ESP32. This library can be found at the following link: `https://github.com/loboris/ESP32_TFT_library`. Now, let's build hardware wiring for the project.

Hardware wiring

If you have the ESP-WROVER-KIT board, you don't need an additional LCD to perform hardware wiring. Otherwise, if you use another LCD module, you can connect the LCD module to the ESP32 board via ESP32 SPI pins. You can see this wiring based on the ESP-WROVER-KIT board datasheet document in Figure 2-7:

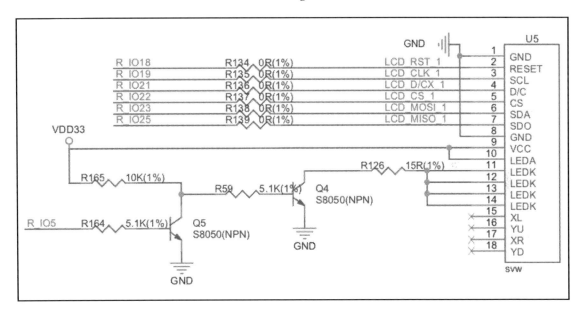

The datasheet can be viewed here:

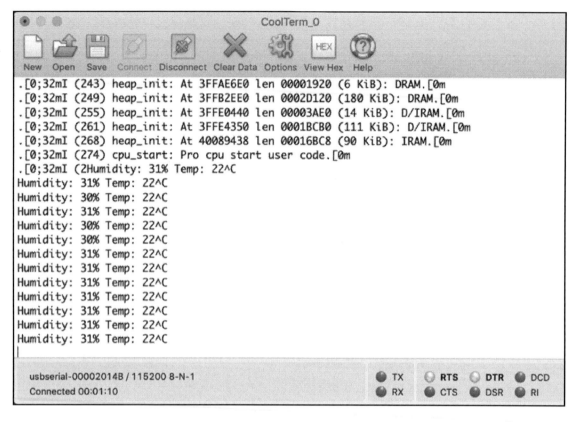

Figure 2-7: Wiring for the LCD module on ESP32

The following is wiring for the ESP32 and LCD module:

- LCD VCC to ESP32 VCC
- LCD GND to ESP32 3.3V
- LCD SCL to ESP32 SPI CLK (IO19)
- LCD SDA to ESP32 MOSI (IO23)
- LCD SDO to ESP32 MISO (IO25)
- LCD CS to ESP32 CS (IO22)
- LCD D/C to ESP32 D/CX (IO21)

Next, we will create a project.

Creating a project

To create a project, follow these steps:

1. Create a project called `lcddemo`. Our main program is the `lcddemo.c` file.
2. Download and copy a project from the TFT library for ESP32: `https://github.com/loboris/ESP32_TFT_library`. This library consists of the TFT LCD driver for ESP32. We can show text and drawings on the TFT LCD.
3. Copy the contents of the components and tools folders into our project. The final result of our project structure can be seen in Figure 2-8:

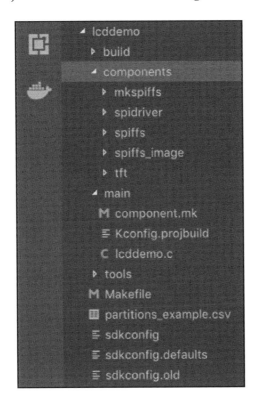

Figure 2-8: Project structure for lcddemo

Now, let's write a program to display circles on the LCD to discuss the project's structure. Ensure that all external libraries are placed on the components folder, as shown in Figure 2-7.

Writing an ESP32 program

To write our program, we need to follow these steps:

1. Modify the `tft_demo.c` file from the TFT library for ESP32. For this, we will use the `circle_demo()` function, as written here:

```
static void circle_demo()
{
  int x, y, r, n;
//In the upper part of the LCD display print the message "CIRCLE DEMO
  disp_header("CIRCLE DEMO");
```

2. Now draw some random circles on the LCD display using the `TFT_drawCircle` function. The circles will be randomly positioned on the screen and will have a random color with the help of the function `random_color()`. After that, the bottom header will be updated with the number of drawn circles (for example, `208 CIRCLES`).

```
uint32_t end_time = clock() + GDEMO_TIME;
n = 0;
while ((clock() < end_time) && (Wait(0))) {
  x = rand_interval(8, dispWin.x2-8);
  y = rand_interval(8, dispWin.y2-8);
  if (x < y) r = rand_interval(2, x/2);
  else r = rand_interval(2, y/2);
  TFT_drawCircle(x,y,r,random_color());
  n++;
}
sprintf(tmp_buff, "%d CIRCLES", n);
update_header(NULL, tmp_buff);
Wait(-GDEMO_INFO_TIME);
```

3. Now is the time to not only draw some circles but also fill to them with colors using the function `TFT_fillCircle()`. In the end, using the same values for x, y and r but different `random_color()` values, the circles will have a different filling and a different edge color.

```
update_header("FILLED CIRCLE", "");
TFT_fillWindow(TFT_BLACK);
end_time = clock() + GDEMO_TIME;
n = 0;
while ((clock() < end_time) && (Wait(0))) {
  x = rand_interval(8, dispWin.x2-8);
```

```
        y = rand_interval(8, dispWin.y2-8);
        if (x < y)  r = rand_interval(2, x/2);
        else r = rand_interval(2, y/2);
        TFT_fillCircle(x,y,r,random_color());
        TFT_drawCircle(x,y,r,random_color());
        n++;
    }
    sprintf(tmp_buff, "%d CIRCLES", n);
    update_header(NULL, tmp_buff);
    Wait(-GDEMO_INFO_TIME);
}
```

4. Next, modify the `tft_demo()` function that calls the `circle_demo()` function:

```
void tft_demo() {

    ...

    // demo
    disp_header("Welcome to ESP32");
    circle_demo();


    while (1) {
        // do nothing
    }
}
```

5. Since we will use some components that are located on `<project>/components`, we should tell the compiler to include these components. We will add the `component.mk` file with our components included, as follows:

```
COMPONENT_SRCDIRS := .
COMPONENT_ADD_INCLUDEDIRS := .
```

6. For the `Makefile` file, we can write these scripts as follows:

```
PROJECT_NAME := lcddemo

EXTRA_CFLAGS += --save-temps

include $(IDF_PATH)/make/project.mk
```

7. Save all files before configuring our project to compile and flash our program into the ESP32 board.

Now that we've created the program, let's configure our board.

Configuring the ESP-WROVER-KIT v4 board

Before we compile and flash our program to the ESP32 board, we should configure our project. In this section, the ESP32 board model is ESP-WROVER-KIT v4. We configure the LCD model and flash size using `menuconfig`. To do so, follow these steps:

1. Open the Terminal and navigate to your project folder.
2. Run `menuconfig` by typing the following command:

```
$ make menuconfig
```

3. You will get a form as shown in Figure 2-9. Select `TFT Display DEMO Configuration` from this form:

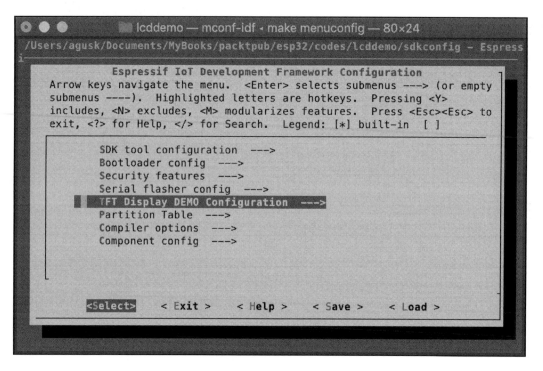

Figure 2-9: Configuring the TFT Display demo

4. You will get a form as shown in Figure 2-10. You can select `Select predefined display configuration`:

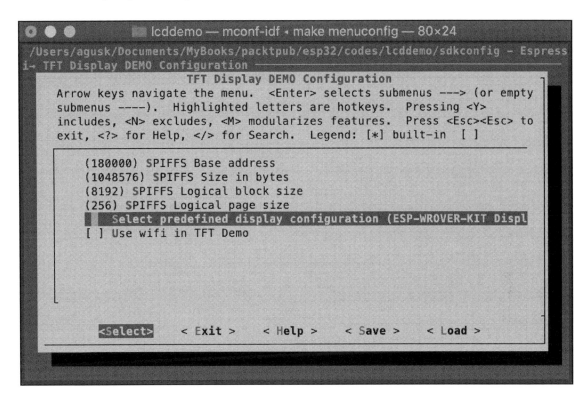

Figure 2-10: Selecting the predefined display configuration

5. You will see a list of TFT modules as shown in Figure 2-11.
6. Since we are using ESP-WROVER-KIT v4, we will select the `ESP-WROVER-KIT Display` option.

7. You can select this option by pressing the *Tab* key on your keyboard:

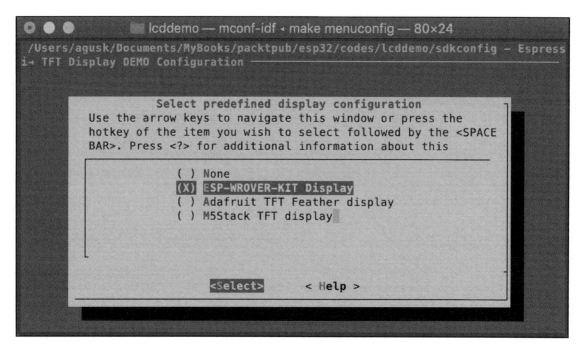

Figure 2-11: Selecting ESP-WROVER-KIT Display

8. Next, we configure the flash size. Navigate back to the main menu as shown in figure 2-9.

9. Select the **Serial flasher config** menu.

10. Then, select the **Flash size** option.

11. After this is selected, you will see a list of flash sizes, as shown in Figure 2-12:

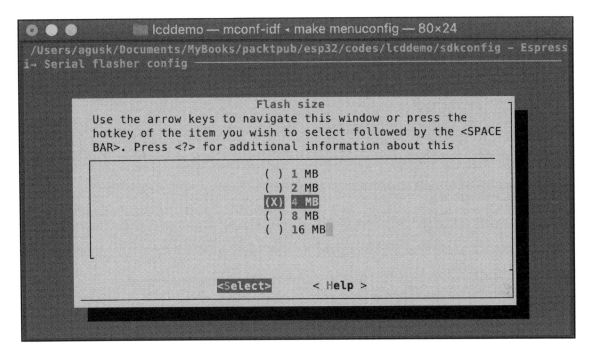

Figure 2-12: Selecting 4MB for flash size

12. Select **4 MB** for flash size.
13. Save this configuration.
14. Select **Exit** to quit `menuconfig`.

After we run `menuconfig`, we will get a config file, `sdkconfig`, as shown in Figure 2-13. Open this file and ensure that this config has a value of `CONFIG_SPIFFS_BASE_ADDR=`
`0x180000`. If you have a value `180000` on that config, you should change it to `0x180000`:

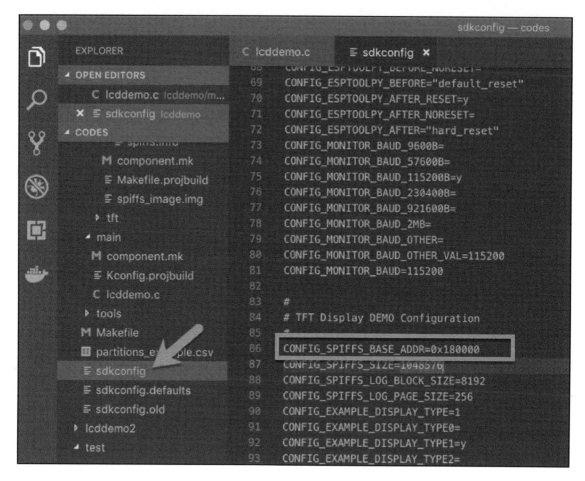

Figure 2-13: Editing the sdkconfig file

Now, your program is ready to compile and run in the next section.

Flashing and running a program

You can compile and flash our program using the following command:

```
$ make flash
```

Make sure that the ESP32 board is connected to your computer.

If the program has been flashed onto the ESP32 board successfully, you should see circles on the LCD. Figure 2-14 shows an example of the program:

Figure 2-14: Displaying circles

So, we have successfully displayed circles on the LCD. Now, let's go a little further and learn to display image files on the LCD.

Displaying image files

If you want to display an image file on the LCD, we should attach picture files in our program. For the demo, we will use picture files from the TFT library for the ESP32 library. These picture files can be found in the `<project>/components/spiffs_image/image/images/` folder:

1. We will continue to work with the `lcddemo` project by copying the `disp_images()` function from the TFT library into the ESP32 library. This function will show the following picture files: `test1.jpg`, `test2.jpg`, and `test4.jpg`.

We will load all of the images from mounted storage:

```
static void disp_images() {
...
    // ** Show scaled (1/8, 1/4, 1/2 size) JPG images
    TFT_jpg_image(CENTER, CENTER, 3, SPIFFS_BASE_PATH"/images/test1.jpg",
NULL, 0);
    Wait(500);

    TFT_jpg_image(CENTER, CENTER, 2, SPIFFS_BASE_PATH"/images/test2.jpg",
NULL, 0);
    Wait(500);

    TFT_jpg_image(CENTER, CENTER, 1, SPIFFS_BASE_PATH"/images/test4.jpg",
NULL, 0);
    Wait(500);
```

Then, we will show JPG images to the LCD using the `TFT_jpg_image()` function:

```
    // ** Show full size JPG image
    tstart = clock();
    TFT_jpg_image(CENTER, CENTER, 0, SPIFFS_BASE_PATH"/images/test3.jpg",
NULL, 0);
    tstart = clock() - tstart;
    if (doprint) printf(" JPG Decode time: %u ms\r\n", tstart);
    sprintf(tmp_buff, "Decode time: %u ms", tstart);
    update_header(NULL, tmp_buff);
    Wait(-GDEMO_INFO_TIME);
```

We will also show JPG images to the LCD using the `TFT_bmp_image()` function:

```
    // ** Show BMP image
    update_header("BMP IMAGE", "");
    for (int scale=5; scale >= 0; scale--) {
      tstart = clock();
      TFT_bmp_image(CENTER, CENTER, scale,
SPIFFS_BASE_PATH"/images/tiger.bmp", NULL, 0);
      tstart = clock() - tstart;

    }
    else if (doprint) printf(" No file system found.\r\n");
```

If there is no picture file, we print No file system found on the Terminal:

```
else if (doprint) printf(" No file system found.\r\n");
```

2. Modify the tft_demo() function to call the disp_images() function, as follows:

```
void tft_demo() {

  . . . . .

  // demo
  // disp_header("Welcome to ESP32");
  // circle_demo();

  disp_images();

  while (1) {
    // do nothing
  }
}
```

3. Save all files.
4. Compile and flash the program into the ESP32 board, as follows:

```
$ make flash
```

5. Compile our picture files as image files:

```
$ make makefs
```

6. Flash our image file into the ESP32 board:

```
$ make flashfs
```

If this succeeds, you will see image files being displayed on the LCD. You can see a sample output in Figure 2-15:

Figure 2-15: Displaying a picture from the file

Now that we've played around with the LCD, let's take the final step toward creating our weather monitoring system.

Making a weather monitoring system

In this section, we'll build a simple weather monitoring system. We'll use the skills that we've learned about, such as reading temperature and humidity from a DHT22 sensor device. Ultimately we'll be able to display the temperature and humidity on the LCD after reading from the sensor device.

Let's begin by creating a project.

Creating a project

To simplify our weather monitoring system project, we will copy the previous project named `lcddemo` and create a project called `weather`. Our main program is `weather.c` on the main folder. You can see a project structure shown in figure 2-16:

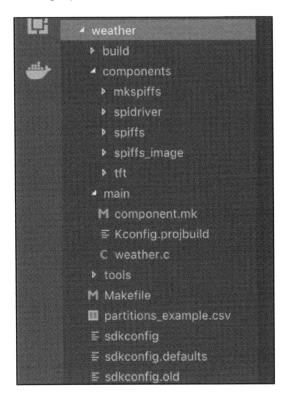

Figure 2-16: Project structure for the weather system

Now, let's move on to hardware wiring.

Hardware wiring

When wiring hardware, we use the same wiring from the `dhtdemo` and `lcddemo` projects.

The DHT22 sensor module is then connected to IO26. Furthermore, our LCD is connected to SPI pins from the ESP32 board.

Writing a program

Let's start writing the program:

1. Copy `lcddemo.c` into the `weather.c` file, and then add the following code to read temperature and humidity from the DHT22 sensor module on the `weather.c` file. Sensor data will then be displayed on the LCD. Add the `dht.h` header file:

```
#include <dht.h>
static const dht_sensor_type_t sensor_type = DHT_TYPE_DHT22;
static const gpio_num_t dht_gpio = 26;
```

2. We define the `weather_system()` function to read temperature and humidity using the `dht_read_data()` function. We display data on the LCD using the `TFT_print()` function, as follows:
   - First we will initialize the sensor variables:

```
void weather_system(){
  int y;

  disp_header("Weather System");

  TFT_setFont(DEFAULT_FONT, NULL);
  _fg = TFT_YELLOW;

    int16_t temperature = 0;
    int16_t humidity = 0;
    char tmp_buff[64];
```

   - Then, we read the DHT sensor using `dht_read_data()` and display it on the LCD using the `TFT_print()` function:

```
if (dht_read_data(sensor_type, dht_gpio, &humidity,
&temperature) == ESP_OK)
    {
      y = 4;
      sprintf(tmp_buff, "Temperature: %d celsius",
temperature/10);
      TFT_print(tmp_buff, 4, y);
      y += TFT_getfontheight() + 4;
```

```
        sprintf(tmp_buff, "Humidity: %d %%",
humidity/10);
        TFT_print(tmp_buff, 4, y);
        update_header(NULL, "Ready");
    }else{
```

- If we don't get sensor data from the device, we give an error message on the header of the LCD screen:

```
    }else{
        update_header(NULL, "Failed to read sensor
data");
    }
```

3. Call the `weather_system()` function into the main entry `app_main()` function:

```
void app_main()
{
    ....

  weather_system();
}
```

4. Save the code.

Now that we have written the program, let's compile and flash this program to the ESP32 board.

Flashing and running

Now that we have written the program that displays the weather data from the sensor, let's display the data on our LCD. You can compile and flash our program into the ESP32 board with the following command:

```
$ make flash
```

If this is successful, you should see temperature and humidity values on the LCD display. You can see my program's output in Figure 2-17:

Figure 2-17: Displaying temperature and humidity on the LCD

We have successfully used the ESP32 board to create a weather monitoring system.

Summary

In this chapter, we looked at a brief introduction that weather systems. Here, we made a simple ESP32 program to sense temperature and humidity using the DHT22 sensor module. Furthermore, we worked with the LCD on the ESP32 board, and were able to access the LCD modules through the ESP32 board. Lastly, we also displayed temperature and humidity data from a sensor to the LCD display. You can now compile and flash any program to your ESP32 board.

In the next chapter, we will learn how to build a simple game on an ESP32 board. We will also cover gaming-embedded systems.

Further reading

To support the information that we have explored in this chapter, I recommend reading the following documents:

- ESP32 MCU datasheet document: `https://www.espressif.com/en/support/download/documents/chips`.
- ESP-IDF Programming Guide document: `https://docs.espressif.com/projects/esp-idf/en/latest/`.
- ESP-WROVER-KIT Getting Started Guide: `https://docs.espressif.com/projects/esp-idf/en/latest/get-started/get-started-wrover-kit.html`.

Building a Simple Game with an Embedded ESP32 Board

3

In this chapter, we will look at developing our own game with an embedded ESP32 board and some embedded modules. Here, we will learn how to work with joystick, buttons, sound, and an LCD.

In this chapter, we will learn about the following topics:

- Game-embedded systems
- Joystick sensor modules
- Working with sound buzzers
- Building a simple embedded game

Technical requirements

Before we begin, make sure you have the following things ready:

- A computer with an OS installed, such as Windows, Linux, or mac
- An ESP32 development board – it is recommended to use the ESP-WROVER-KIT v4 board from Espressif

Introducing game-embedded systems

You will be familiar with the Game Boy, an 8-bit handheld game console developed by Nintendo. This console includes joystick, buttons, and an LCD. A joystick is used to move an object from one place to another, while buttons are usually used for actions such as firing and jumping.

A game embedded system is described in a general sense in figure 3-1. As well as the features just mentioned, having a sound system increases a game's potential in terms of entertainment. For this purpose, we need a sound actuator such as a speaker to generate sounds for the game:

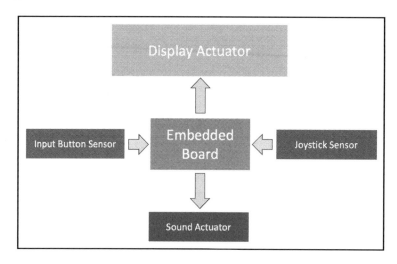

Figure 3-1: A general architecture of an embedded system for gaming

Next, we will review a joystick sensor module.

Introducing the joystick sensor module

If you have experience with playing games on consoles such as PlayStation or Xbox, you will be familiar with using joystick control to manage game movements and perform various actions. An analog joystick usually consists of two potentiometers. This sensor generates 2D direction points.

There are many cheap analog joystick sensors available in online electronics stores such as AliExpress and Alibaba. One of the analog joystick models is Thumb Joystick from SparkFun, found at the following link: https://www.sparkfun.com/products/9032. You can see this device in figure 3-2:

Figure 3-2: a simple joystick sensor

An analog joystick usually has five pins: VCC, GND, Vx, Vy, and SW. The Vx and Vy pins represent direction values from the device.

Another option is to use a joystick module kit. This is a complete kit that you use directly on your board. You can find the SparkFun Joystick Shield Kit at the following link: `https://www.sparkfun.com/products/9760`. This form can be seen in figure 3-3:

Figure 3-3: The joystick module from SparkFun

Technically, an analog joystick can be defined as in figure 3-4. The movement of an analog joystick is 2D. If we move the joystick to the left, we will get Vx approaching zero. Otherwise, we can perform for Vy, as shown here:

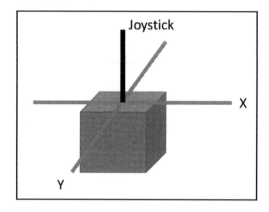

Figure 3-4: The joystick navigation

Next, we'll implement the ESP32 program with the joystick sensor.

Working with the joystick sensor module

Connecting an analog joystick to the ESP32 is easy. You can just connect this device to the analog pins. The ESP32 has two ADC1 and ADC2 pins, with some channels. You can find the analog pins with their channels on the ESP32 in figure 3-5:

Signal	Pin
ADC1_CH0	SENSOR_VP
ADC1_CH3	SENSOR_VN
ADC1_CH4	IO32
ADC1_CH5	IO33
ADC1_CH6	IO34
ADC1_CH7	IO35
ADC2_CH0	IO4
ADC2_CH1	IO0
ADC2_CH2	IO2
ADC2_CH3	IO15
ADC2_CH4	IO13
ADC2_CH5	IO12
ADC2_CH6	IO14
ADC2_CH7	IO27
ADC2_CH8	IO25
ADC2_CH9	IO26

Figure 3-5: ADC pinout on ESP32

 Some ADC2 pins are used for internal devices such as Wi-Fi. For the ESP-WROVER-KIT board, GPIO 0, 2, 4, and 15 cannot be used for ADC due to external connections for different purposes.

Wiring

In this section, we'll perform hardware wiring between the ESP32 and analog joystick. For demo purposes, I will use the ESP-WROVER-KIT v4.1 board. We can connect our analog joystick with the ESP32 on the following wiring:

- Analog joystick 5V is connected to ESP32 5V
- Analog joystick GND is connected to ESP32 GND
- Analog joystick Vx is connected to ESP32 IO35 (ADC1 channel 7)
- Analog joystick Vy is connected to ESP32 IO15 (ADC2 channel 3)

You can see the hardware wiring in figure 3-6, as follows:

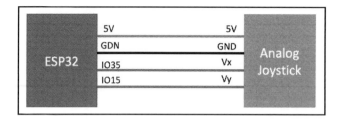

Figure 3-6: The wiring for the ESP32 and analog joystick

Next, we write a project for the analog joystick and ESP32.

Creating a project

In this section, we will create a project called joystickdemo. You can follow the instructions in Chapter 2, *Making Visual Data and Animation on an LCD, Weather project*, to create a project. Figure 3-7 shows our project structure:

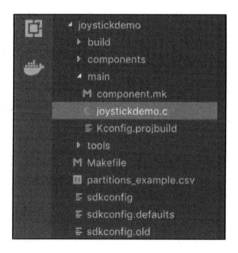

Figure 3-7: The project structure for joystickdemo

Our main program is the joystickdemo.c file. We can copy the file content from weather.c from Chapter 2, *Making Visual Data and Animation on an LCD*, in the *Weather Project section*.

Next, we'll write a program on the joystickdemo.c file.

Writing the program

Our program will read the analog joystick positions, x and y, through the ADC pins. Then, we display these positions on the LCD.

Firstly, we modify the `tft_demo()` function. We call `joystick_demo()` in the `tft_demo()` function as follows:

```
void tft_demo() {

  ...


  joystick_demo();

}
```

We declare the `joystick_demo()` function to read the analog joystick via ADC. The result of the ADC measurement is displayed on the LCD. To retrieve analog data from ADC1, we perform the following steps:

- Set ADC bit length using the `adc1_config_width()` function
- Set ADC attenuation with the `adc1_config_channel_atten()` function
- To get ADC value, we can use the `adc1_get_raw()` function

For ADC2, we don't need to call the `adc1_config_width()` function. Instead, we call `adc2_get_raw()` with the ADC bit-length parameter.

The following are the complete codes for the `joystick_demo()` function:

```
static void joystick_demo()
{
  int y;
  TFT_resetclipwin();
  adc1_config_width(ADC_WIDTH_12Bit);

  adc1_config_channel_atten(ADC1_CHANNEL_7, ADC_ATTEN_11db);
  adc2_config_channel_atten(ADC2_CHANNEL_3, ADC_ATTEN_11db);
  disp_header("JOYSTIK DEMO");
  update_header(NULL, "Move your joystick");
  char tmp_buff[64];
  int joyX, joyY;
  while(1){
    joyX = adc1_get_raw(ADC1_CHANNEL_7);
    adc2_get_raw(ADC2_CHANNEL_3, ADC_WIDTH_12Bit, &joyY);
    y = 4;
```

```
        sprintf(tmp_buff, "x: %d y: %d ", joyX,joyY);
        TFT_print(tmp_buff, 4, y);
        vTaskDelay(500 / portTICK_PERIOD_MS);

        // clear text
        TFT_clearStringRect(4,y,tmp_buff);
        tmp_buff[0]='\0';
    }
}
```

Save the program.

After doing this, we compile and flash this program onto the ESP32 board.

Running the program

You can compile and flash the `joystickdemo` program onto the ESP32. To do this, just type this command:

```
$ make flash
```

Make sure the ESP32 serial port is correct.

After the screen is flashed, you can see the LCD display on the screen. Try to move the dot position of the screen by changing direction using the analog joystick. Figure 3-8 shows a sample of the program output on the LCD:

Figure 3-8: A sample of the program output on the LCD for the joystickdemo project

You can see this demo on my YouTube account at the following link: `https://youtu.be/lIVEkXa16Fg`

Next, we'll learn how to work with a sound buzzer on the ESP33 board.

Working with a sound buzzer

In this section, we'll work with sound. Most games usually use music to provide sound background. For a simple sound device, we can use sound buzzer devices. We can use a PC-mountable mini-speaker - PC Mount (12mm, 2.048kHz) from SparkFun, found at the following link: `https://www.sparkfun.com/products/7950`. You can see this in Figure 3-9, and you can also find some other sound buzzer models with low prices at AliExpress:

Figure 3-9: Mini Speaker - PC Mount

Next, we connect the sound buzzer to the ESP32 board.

Connecting the sound buzzer with the ESP32

A sound buzzer has two pins. One pin is connected to the GPIO and the other is connected to the GND. We connect a sound buzzer to the ESP32 IO27 as follows:

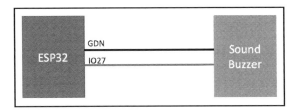

Figure 3-10: The wiring for the sound buzzer and ESP32

Next, we write a program to access the sound buzzer device.

Writing a program for the sound buzzer with the ESP32

To do this, we create a project called buzzer. You can see that the project structure in figure 3-11. The buzzer.c file is our main program:

Figure 3-11: Project structure for the buzzer

Firstly, we declare all required header files and define IO27 for the sound buzzer:

```
#include <stdio.h>
#include "freertos/FreeRTOS.h"
#include "freertos/task.h"
#include "driver/gpio.h"
#include "sdkconfig.h"

#define BUZZER 27
```

We also define the main entry on the app_main() function. This function will execute the buzzer_task() function:

```
void app_main()
{
    xTaskCreate(&buzzer_task, "buzzer_task", configMINIMAL_STACK_SIZE,
NULL, 5, NULL);
}
```

Technically, we generate sound on the sensor by giving HIGH on IO27. We can use the `gpio_set_level()` function for this. The following is an implementation of the `buzzer_task()` function:

```
void buzzer_task(void *pvParameter)
{
    // set gpio and its direction
    gpio_pad_select_gpio(BUZZER);
    gpio_set_direction(BUZZER, GPIO_MODE_OUTPUT);

    int sounding = 1;
    while(1) {

        if(sounding==1){
            gpio_set_level(BUZZER, 1);
            sounding = 0;
        }
        else {
            gpio_set_level(BUZZER, 0);
            sounding = 1;
        }
        vTaskDelay(1000 / portTICK_PERIOD_MS);
    }
}
```

Once you have saved this program, you can compile and flash the program onto the ESP32 board.

When this has successfully completed, you should hear a sound from the buzzer device.

Demo – building a simple embedded game

In this section, we will develop a simple game. To do this, we integrate our previous experiences using the LCD, analog joystick, and sound buzzer. We will build a ball game here. For the implementation of this game project, we use the the ESP-WROVER-KIT for ESP32 board.

Let's start!

The game scenario

Each game has a scenario. Some games also define some levels for users. In this project, we'll make a simple game scenario. We define our game flowchart in Figure 3-12, as follows:

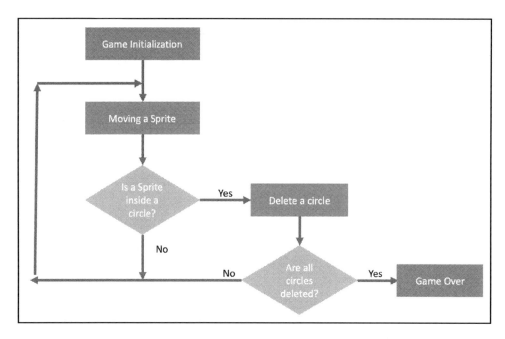

Figure 3-12: A game scenario for a ball-hitting game

We can build a game scenario as follows:

1. Initialize a game by populating a circle with a different radius. These circles are represented as sprites.
2. Set our ball sprite on a certain coordinate.
3. The user can move the ball sprite using the analog joystick.
4. If our ball is inside a circle, we turn on the sound buzzer for a few seconds.
5. If not, we don't do anything.
6. If all circles are deleted, the game will be completed. Game over will be displayed on the LCD.

Next, we perform wiring and writing a program for the game.

Hardware wiring

We'll integrate our wiring from the `joystickdemo` and `buzzer` projects. You can check them in the previous section of this chapter.

Developing the game program

Now, you can create a project called `game`. You can copy a project from `Chapter 2`, *Making Visual Data and Animation on an LCD*, Weather Project. Figure 3-13 shows our project structure:

Figure 3-13. Project structure for game.

To detect collision between our sprite and circle sprites, we can use a simple method. This involves calculating the distance between our position and circle center point. Then, we compare the point-to-circle distance and circle radius. If our distance is lower than the circle radius, this means that our sprite hits the circle. This is demonstrated in Figure 3-14:

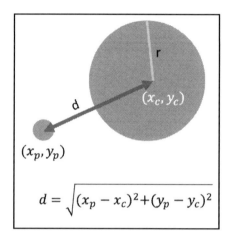

Figure 3-14: A formula to detect a sprite collision

Now, we modify the `tft_demo()` function codes on `game.c`. We call the `game_demo()` function on the end of the code lines from the `tft_demo()` function, as follows:

```
void tft_demo() {

    ...
    game_demo();

}
```

Our game scenario is implemented in the `game_demo()` function.

1. Firstly, we initialize our circle sprites, ADC, and sound buzzer, as follows:

```
static void game_demo()
{
    int x, y, r, i, n;
    n = 10;
    Circle_Sprite circles[n];

    // initialize ADC
    adc1_config_width(ADC_WIDTH_12Bit);
        adc1_config_channel_atten(ADC1_CHANNEL_7, ADC_ATTEN_11db);
        adc2_config_channel_atten(ADC2_CHANNEL_3, ADC_ATTEN_11db);
```

```
// set gpio and its direction for buzzer
  gpio_pad_select_gpio(BUZZER);
  gpio_set_direction(BUZZER, GPIO_MODE_OUTPUT);

// initialize screen
TFT_resetclipwin();
disp_header("Circle Game Demo");
update_header(NULL, "Move your joystick to circle");
```

2. We generate a random position and radius for all circles, and save all circle data in the circles[] variable, as follows:

```
// generate circles
for(i=0;i<n;i++){
  x = rand_interval(16, dispWin.x2-16);
  y = rand_interval(32, dispWin.y2-32);

  r = rand_interval(8, 16);
  color_t c = random_color();
  TFT_fillCircle(x,y,r,c);
  circles[i].x = x;
  circles[i].y = y;
  circles[i].r = r;
  circles[i].deleted = 0;
  circles[i].color = c;
}
```

3. We show our sprite with a current position of x=100 and y=100:

```
int joyX, joyY;
int running = 1;
r = 8;
int curr_x = 100, curr_y = 100;
int cx = 151, cy = 212;

TFT_fillCircle(curr_x,curr_y,r,TFT_RED);
vTaskDelay(1000 / portTICK_PERIOD_MS);
TFT_drawCircle(curr_x,curr_y,r,TFT_BLACK);

char tmp_buff[64];
int sound = 0;
```

4. Now, we perform looping with while() syntax. For this, we read the analog joystick and change our sprite position based on the analog joystick input.

We also detect whether our sprite hits or not by calling the check_insideCircle() function. If it does, we delete our circle from the screen.

If our sprite moves to out of the boundaries of the LCD, we put it on the end of the LCD position by setting `curr_x` and `curr_y`.

5. Lastly, if all circles are hit, we finish our game:

```
while(running){
    joyX = adc1_get_raw(ADC1_CHANNEL_7);
    adc2_get_raw(ADC2_CHANNEL_3,ADC_WIDTH_12Bit, &joyY);

    joyX = map_to_screen(joyX,0,4095,0,dispWin.x2);
    joyY = map_to_screen(joyY,0,4095,0,dispWin.y2);
    // validate point to screen
    curr_x = curr_x + joyX - cx;
    curr_y = curr_y + joyY - cy;
```

Check if the cursor is outside of our screen and adjust the values to keep it on the screen.

```
    if(curr_x<8)
        curr_x = 8;
    if(curr_x>(dispWin.x2-8))
        curr_x = dispWin.x2 - 8;
    if(curr_y<32)
        curr_y = 32;
    if(curr_y>(dispWin.y2-32))
        curr_y = dispWin.y2-32;
```

6. Looping over all circles that we keep in the `circles[]` array and skipping the ones that were previously deleted, we need to check if our ball is inside the target circle. This is done by the `check_insideCircle()` function. If that is the case, based on the stored coordinates, we will fill the circle with black (`TFT_BLACK`), the same color as our background, thus giving the impression that the circle has disappeared.

```
    // check a ball inside a circle
    for(i=0;i<n;i++){
        if(circles[i].deleted == 1)
            continue;
        if(check_insideCircle(curr_x,curr_y,circles[i])==1){
            gpio_set_level(BUZZER, 1);
            sound = 1;
            circles[i].deleted = 1;
            TFT_fillCircle(circles[i].x,circles[i].y,circles[i].r,TFT_BLACK);
            break;
        }
    }
    TFT_fillCircle(curr_x,curr_y,r,TFT_RED);
```

7. Change the color to yellow and then to black again. Then, play a short beep on buzzer.

```
_fg = TFT_YELLOW;
sprintf(tmp_buff, "x: %d y: %d ", curr_x,curr_y);
TFT_print(tmp_buff, 4, 4);
vTaskDelay(200 / portTICK_PERIOD_MS);
TFT_fillCircle(curr_x,curr_y,r,TFT_BLACK);
_fg = TFT_BLACK;
TFT_print(tmp_buff, 4, 4);
if(sound==1){
    gpio_set_level(BUZZER, 0);
    sound = 0;
}
```

If it is the last circle on the screen, then it is the end of the game since all the circles were hit.

```
// check if finished
int nn = 0;
for(i=0;i<n;i++){
    if(circles[i].deleted == 1)
        nn++;
}
if(nn==n)
    break;
}
```

8. At the finishing stage, we show Game Over on the LCD using the TFT_print() function, as follows:

```
TFT_resetclipwin();
disp_header("ESP32 Game DEMO");
TFT_setFont(COMIC24_FONT, NULL);
int tempy = TFT_getfontheight() + 4;
_fg = TFT_ORANGE;
TFT_print("ESP32-", CENTER, (dispWin.y2-dispWin.y1)/2 - tempy);
TFT_setFont(UBUNTU16_FONT, NULL);
_fg = TFT_CYAN;
TFT_print("Game Over", CENTER, LASTY+tempy);
tempy = TFT_getfontheight() + 4;
TFT_setFont(DEFAULT_FONT, NULL);
while(1){

}
}
```

We can implement object collision in the check_insideCircle() function. For this, we will use a math formula from Figure 3-14. You can write codes for the check_insideCircle() function as follows:

```
int check_insideCircle(int x, int y, Circle_Sprite sp){
  int d = sqrt(pow(x-sp.x,2)+pow(y-sp.y,2));

  if(d<=sp.r)
    return 1;
  else{
    int rr = d - sp.r - 8;
    if(rr<=0)
      return 1;
    else
      return 0;
  }
}
```

9. Save this program.

You are now ready to compile and flash the program onto the ESP32 board.

Playing the game

Compile and flash our game project onto the ESP32.

To apply a game, you move your sprite to hit all circles. If all circles are hit, a game will finish. You can see a form of the game program in Figure 3-15:

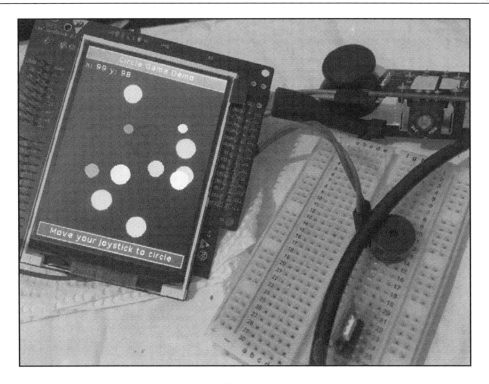

Figure 3-15: A ball-hitting game

I have recorded how to play this game on my YouTube account. You can see it at this link: https://youtu.be/sXmZ1pJ_l1E.

Summary

We have learned how to work with an analog joystick to control movement, as well as exploring a simple sound device with a sound buzzer and developing a simple game. We hit all circles in order to finish the game.

In the next chapter, we will make a sensor-monitoring logger.

Building a Sensor Monitoring Logger

4

Storing sensor data in external storage can make our IoT system more reliable. In this chapter, we will explore how to store sensor data in external storage, such as SD cards and microSD cards.

In this chapter, we will cover the following topics:

- Introducing the sensor-monitoring logger
- Accessing microSD cards from the ESP32
- Storing sensor data in external storage
- Building a simple sensor monitoring logger

Technical requirements

Before we begin, make sure you have the following things ready:

- A computer with an OS installed, such as Windows, Linux, or macOS.
- An ESP32 development board. The ESP-WROVER-KIT v4 board from Espressif is recommended for this.

Introducing the sensor monitoring logger

A logging system is a system that can write data and information.

Data and information could include sensor data, system events, and error messages. All data and information is usually stored in external storage such as SD cards, microSD cards, or on a hard disk.

In general, a logging system can be described as in the following figure. An MCU with sensor devices attached can sense things such as temperature and humidity. This sensor data can also be stored in external storage:

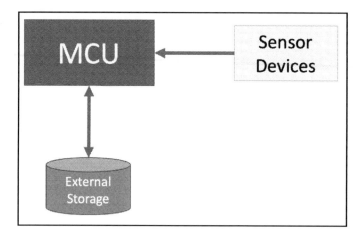

Figure 4-1: A general model for a logging system

In this chapter, we explore how to work with external storage from an ESP32 board. We will build a simple logging system to store sensor data in external storage.

Accessing a microSD card from the ESP32

To work with external storage such as SD and microSD cards, we should have an SD/microSD card breakout device. We attach this breakout device into the ESP32 board through SPI and SDMC pins.

SD/microSD card breakout devices are widely available in electronics stores. For example, you can use the SparkFun microSD Transflash Breakout. You can attach a microSD card into this breakout, which you can find at SparkFun's website: https://www.slparkfun. com/products/544. A form of the SparkFun microSD Transflash Breakout is shown in the following photo:

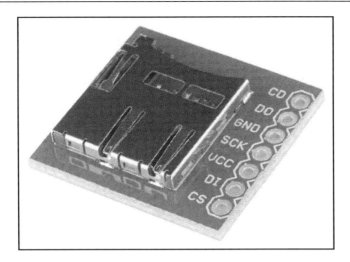

Figure 4-2: SparkFun microSD Transflash Breakout

If you prefer to use an SD card with the ESP32, you can choose a breakout device for an SD card. For example, you can use the SparkFun SD/MMC Card Breakout. You can get this device on the official website: `https://www.sparkfun.com/products/12941`. A form of the SparkFun SD/MMC Card Breakout can be seen, here:

Figure 4-3: SparkFun SD/MMC Card Breakout

Next, we will develop a program for the ESP32 to access microSD cards.

Demo – accessing microSD cards from the ESP32

In this section, we develop a simple program to access a microSD card from the ESP32. For the demo, I use the ESP-WROVER-KIT v4 board. Fortunately, the ESP-WROVER-KIT v4 board has a built-in microSD card breakout that is connected to SDMMC pins.

Your ESP32 board should be connected to the microSD card breakout to perform this demo. You also need a microSD storage card with a small size, such as 1 GB, 2 GB or 4 GB. Your microSD card storage should be formatted as FAT.

Our demo scenario is aimed at creating a file named test.txt on a microSD card. Then, we read the content of the test.txt file and print this to the serial Terminal.

Now, you can create an ESP32 project called sdcard. Our main project file is sdcard.c and is located in the main folder. Firstly, we declare all required header files, including sdmmc and sdspi:

```
#include <stdio.h>
#include <string.h>
#include <sys/unistd.h>
#include <sys/stat.h>
#include "esp_err.h"
#include "esp_log.h"
#include "esp_vfs_fat.h"
#include "driver/sdmmc_host.h"
#include "driver/sdspi_host.h"
#include "sdmmc_cmd.h"
```

Depending on your microSD card breakout model, you can access this breakout via SPI or SDMMC. If you use an SPI connection on a microSD card breakout, you should define SPI pins on our codes. Declare the USE_SPI_MODE syntax on these codes, as follows:

```
// To enable SPI mode, uncomment the following line:
// #define USE_SPI_MODE


#ifdef USE_SPI_MODE
#define PIN_NUM_MISO 2
#define PIN_NUM_MOSI 15
#define PIN_NUM_CLK 14
#define PIN_NUM_CS 13
#endif //USE_SPI_MODE
```

Change the SPI pins with your hardware configuration to use the SPI connection on a microSD card. The pins include `PIN_NUM_MISO`, `PIN_NUM_MOSI`, `PIN_NUM_CLK`, and `PIN_NUM_CS`.

Now, we should write code for the main entry on the `app_main()` function. We initialize our GPIO for microSD via SPI or SDMMC:

```
void app_main(void)
{
    ESP_LOGI(TAG, "Initializing SD card");

#ifndef USE_SPI_MODE
    ESP_LOGI(TAG, "Using SDMMC peripheral");
    sdmmc_host_t host = SDMMC_HOST_DEFAULT();
    sdmmc_slot_config_t slot_config = SDMMC_SLOT_CONFIG_DEFAULT();

    gpio_set_pull_mode(15, GPIO_PULLUP_ONLY); // CMD, needed in 4- and 1-
line modes
    gpio_set_pull_mode(2, GPIO_PULLUP_ONLY); // D0, needed in 4- and 1-line
modes
    gpio_set_pull_mode(4, GPIO_PULLUP_ONLY); // D1, needed in 4-line mode
only
    gpio_set_pull_mode(12, GPIO_PULLUP_ONLY); // D2, needed in 4-line mode
only
    gpio_set_pull_mode(13, GPIO_PULLUP_ONLY); // D3, needed in 4- and 1-
line modes

#else
    ESP_LOGI(TAG, "Using SPI peripheral");

    sdmmc_host_t host = SDSPI_HOST_DEFAULT();
    sdspi_slot_config_t slot_config = SDSPI_SLOT_CONFIG_DEFAULT();
    slot_config.gpio_miso = PIN_NUM_MISO;
    slot_config.gpio_mosi = PIN_NUM_MOSI;
    slot_config.gpio_sck = PIN_NUM_CLK;
    slot_config.gpio_cs = PIN_NUM_CS;
#endif //USE_SPI_MODE
```

We continue to mount our microSD into the ESP32 using `esp_vfs_fat_sdmmc_mount()`. We mount our microSD storage as the `"/sdcard"` driver. If we succeed in mounting microSD storage into the ESP32, we can print our microSD storage into the Terminal using `sdmmc_card_print_info()`:

```
    // Options for mounting the filesystem.
    esp_vfs_fat_sdmmc_mount_config_t mount_config = {
        .format_if_mount_failed = false,
        .max_files = 5,
```

```
        .allocation_unit_size = 16 * 1024
};

sdmmc_card_t* card;
esp_err_t ret = esp_vfs_fat_sdmmc_mount("/sdcard", &host, &slot_config,
&mount_config, &card);

if (ret != ESP_OK) {
    if (ret == ESP_FAIL) {
        ESP_LOGE(TAG, "Failed to mount filesystem. "
            "If you want the card to be formatted, set
format_if_mount_failed = true.");
    } else {
        ESP_LOGE(TAG, "Failed to initialize the card (%s). "
            "Make sure SD card lines have pull-up resistors in place.",
esp_err_to_name(ret));
    }
    return;
}

// Card has been initialized, print its properties
sdmmc_card_print_info(stdout, card);
```

At this stage, our program has mounted the microSD storage, so we can access it. We use normal file operation in C program, as well as the `fopen()`, `fprintf()`, and `fclose()` functions for file manipulation.

The following is a program sample to create a file, write data into the file, and read the content of a file:

```
// Use POSIX and C standard library functions to work with files.
// First create a file.
ESP_LOGI(TAG, "Opening file");
FILE* f = fopen("/sdcard/test.txt", "w");
if (f == NULL) {
    ESP_LOGE(TAG, "Failed to open file for writing");
    return;
}
ESP_LOGI(TAG, "Writing data into a file");
fprintf(f, "Hello %s!\n", card->cid.name);
fprintf(f, "This is the content 1\n");
fprintf(f, "This is the content 2\n");
fclose(f);
ESP_LOGI(TAG, "File written");

// Open renamed file for reading
ESP_LOGI(TAG, "Reading file");
f = fopen("/sdcard/test.txt", "r");
```

```
if (f == NULL) {
    ESP_LOGE(TAG, "Failed to open file for reading");
    return;
}
char line[64];
while (fgets(line, sizeof(line), f) != NULL){
    ESP_LOGI(TAG, "Read from file: '%s'", line);
}
fclose(f);
```

Lastly, you should unmount the microSD storage from the ESP32 if you don't access the file. We can call the `esp_vfs_fat_sdmmc_unmount()` function to unmount a microSD storage card:

```
esp_vfs_fat_sdmmc_unmount();
ESP_LOGI(TAG, "Card unmounted");
```

Save our program on `sdcard.c`.

Compile and flash our project, `sdcard`, onto the ESP32 board. For testing, open a serial application such as CoolTerm, and connect to the ESP32 board. You should see file operation information in the serial Terminal, as shown in the following screenshot:

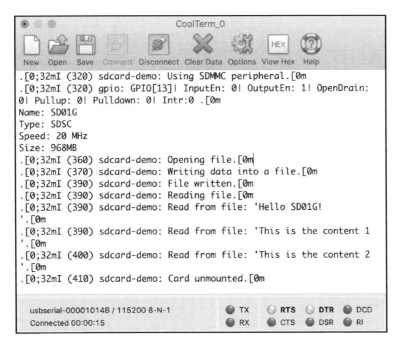

Figure 4-4: Program output from the sdcard program

If you unplug the microSD storage from the ESP32 board to your computer, you should see the TEST.TXT file in the microSD storage. The contents of the TEST.TXT file should be as follows:

```
Hello <sdcard_id>
This is the content 1
This is the content 2
```

<sdcard_id> is your storage ID name.

Storing sensor data on a microSD card

Technically, we can store any data of a certain file type on an SD card and microSD card. We can also store sensor data in external storage.

For demo purposes, we sense temperature and humidity with the DHT sensor. We use the same wiring from the dhtdemo project in Chapter 2, *Making Visual Data and Animation on an LCD*. Our scenario is to sense temperature and humidity and then store them in microSD storage.

We clone our previous project, sdcard. Then, we change to a new project by naming it sdcarddht. We should then rename the main program file sdcard.c to sdcarddht.c. We modify codes on file operations to read temperature and humidity from DHT by calling the dht_read_data() function. After obtaining sensor data, we store it into a file named sensor.txt:

```
        ESP_LOGE(TAG, "Reading sensor data");

        if (dht_read_data(sensor_type, dht_gpio, &humidity, &temperature)
== ESP_OK)
        {
            printf("Humidity: %d%% Temp: %d^C\n", humidity / 10,
temperature / 10);
            FILE* f = fopen("/sdcard/sensor.txt", "a");
            if (f == NULL) {
                ESP_LOGE(TAG, "Failed to open file for writing");
                return;
            }
            fprintf(f, "Humidity: %d%% Temp: %d^C\n", humidity / 10,
temperature / 10);
            fclose(f);
        }
        else
            printf("Could not read data from sensor\n");
```

Now, save the code.

Now, you can compile and flash a program into the ESP32 board. Open a serial application to see the program output from the `sdcardht` project. The following screenshot shows a sample of the program output from the `sdcardht` project:

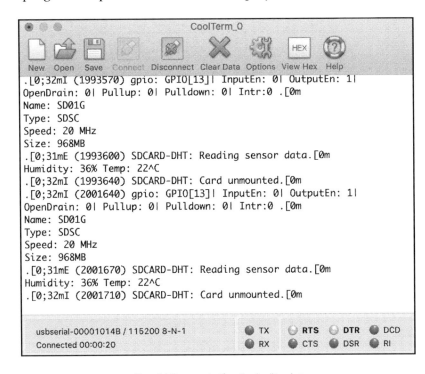

Figure 4-5: Program output from the sdcardht project

Project – building a sensor monitoring logger

In this section, we build a sensor monitoring logger with an ESP32 and a DHT module. Here, we will store all sensor data in a CSV file on the microSD storage. We can visualize our sensor data from the CSV file using a visual tool such as Excel.

Let's start!

Designing our program

Technically, we can develop our logger project by designing a flow chart, as shown in the following diagram. We use a deep-sleep feature from the ESP32 chip to work with sleep mode:

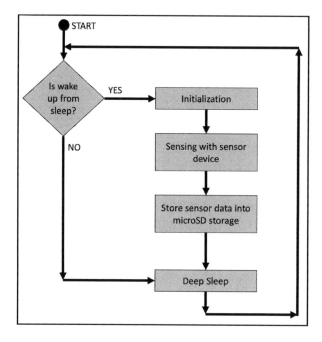

Figure 4-6: Program design for the logger project

We can start implementing our program scenario based on the flowchart in figure 4-6 as follows:

- We will check if the program runs after sleep mode or not.
- If yes, we perform our sensing and storing sensor data. If not, we perform the sleep mode operation.
- We initialize our sensor and microSD storage on the ESP32 board.
- We store sensor data in microSD storage after sensing temperature and humidity with the DHT module.
- After storing the sensor data, the program will enter sleep mode.

In this project, we use a timer to wake our program from sleep mode.

Writing the program

We can clone our previous project, `sdcardht`, in order to make our demonstration easy. We rename the old project with a new name called logger. Our main program file is `logger.c`.

1. Firstly, we declare our `sleep_enter_time` for sleep mode operation:

```
static RTC_DATA_ATTR struct timeval sleep_enter_time;
```

We can calculate sleep duration by comparing the starting time and the current time. We will put the sleep duration value on the `sleep_time_ms` variable:

```
struct timeval now;
gettimeofday(&now, NULL);
int sleep_time_ms = (now.tv_sec - sleep_enter_time.tv_sec) * 1000 +
(now.tv_usec - sleep_enter_time.tv_usec) / 1000;
```

2. To check if our program runs after sleep mode or not, we can use the `esp_sleep_get_wakeup_cause()` function. We will get `ESP_SLEEP_WAKEUP_TIMER` if our program wakes up from sleep mode.

3. Then, we perform sensing using the DHT module, and store sensor data on the microSD storage:

```
switch (esp_sleep_get_wakeup_cause()) {
    case ESP_SLEEP_WAKEUP_TIMER: {
        printf("Wake up from timer. Time spent in deep sleep: %dms\n",
sleep_time_ms);

        // Options for mounting the filesystem.
        esp_vfs_fat_sdmmc_mount_config_t mount_config = {
            .format_if_mount_failed = false,
            .max_files = 5,
            .allocation_unit_size = 16 * 1024
        };
```

4. After the ESP32 is started after a deep sleep, the information about the card needs to be set up again in variable `mount_config`. The next step is to mount the `"/sdcard"` mount point and to ensure that the operation is completed without any errors. In case of errors, depending on the error, some helper messages will be printed on the serial terminal.

```
sdmmc_card_t* card;
esp_err_t ret = esp_vfs_fat_sdmmc_mount("/sdcard", &host,
&slot_config, &mount_config, &card);

if (ret != ESP_OK) {
    if (ret == ESP_FAIL) {
        printf("Failed to mount filesystem. "
            "If you want the card to be formatted, set
format_if_mount_failed = true.\n");
    } else {
        printf("Failed to initialize the card (%s). "
            "Make sure SD card lines have pull-up resistors in
place.\n", esp_err_to_name(ret));
    }
    return;
}

// Card has been initialized, print its properties
sdmmc_card_print_info(stdout, card);

printf("Reading sensor data\n");
```

5. Now that the card is mounted without any errors, we can read the values from the DHT sensor. Open the file `"/sdcard/logger.csv"` in the append mode (see the second parameter of the `fopen` function), taking care not to overwrite the previous values, and write the current humidity and temperature in the file by using the `fprintf()` function.

Now that a new record is added to the file `"/sdcard/logger.csv"`, we can close the file by calling the function `fclose` and passing the file descriptor.

```
if (dht_read_data(sensor_type, dht_gpio, &humidity,
&temperature) == ESP_OK)
{
    printf("Humidity: %d%% Temp: %d^C\n", humidity / 10,
temperature / 10);
    FILE* f = fopen("/sdcard/logger.csv", "a");
    if (f == NULL) {
        printf("Failed to open file for writing\n");
        return;
```

```
                    }
                    fprintf(f, "%d,%d\n", humidity / 10, temperature / 10);
                    fclose(f);
                }
                else
                    printf("Could not read data from sensor\n");


                // All done, unmount partition and disable SDMMC or SPI
peripheral
```

6. Now that we have the latest reading stored on our file on the SD card and the file is closed, we should unmount the card and prepare it for another deep sleep period. After that, the same process will be done repeatedly.

```
                esp_vfs_fat_sdmmc_unmount();
                printf("Card unmounted\n");

                break;
            }
            case ESP_SLEEP_WAKEUP_UNDEFINED:
            default:
                printf("Not a deep sleep reset\n");
        }
        vTaskDelay(1000 / portTICK_PERIOD_MS);
```

To enable our program to enter sleep mode, we call `esp_deep_sleep_start()`. Before calling `esp_deep_sleep_start()`, we set our wake-up timer. In this program, we wake up every 20 seconds:

```
        const int wakeup_time_sec = 20;
        printf("Enabling timer wakeup, %ds\n", wakeup_time_sec);
        esp_sleep_enable_timer_wakeup(wakeup_time_sec * 1000000);

        esp_deep_sleep_start();
```

7. Save all programs.

Running the program

Now, you can compile and upload the logger project onto the ESP32 board. If done, you can use the serial application to see the program output. The following screenshot shows an example of the program output from the `logger` project:

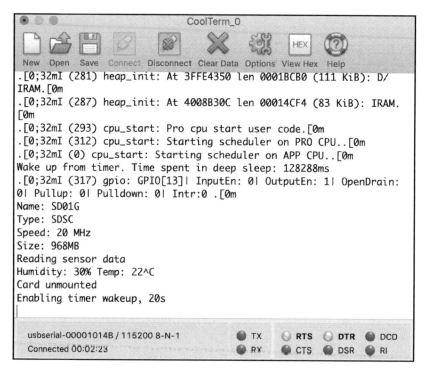

Figure 4-7: Program output from the logger project

The logger project will generate a `logger.csv` file. You can use Microsoft Excel to visualize the `logger.csv` file. You can see a sample visualization of the sensor data in the following screenshot:

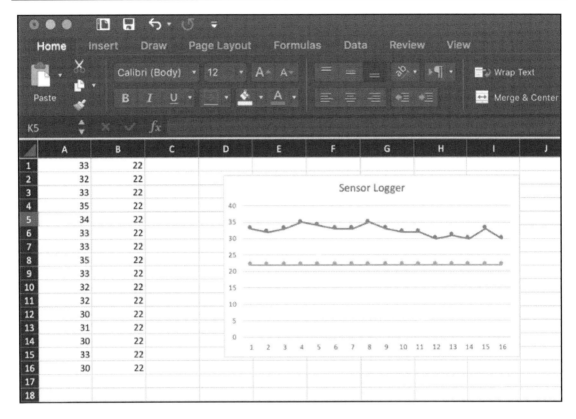

Figure 4-8: Visualizing sensor data with Microsoft Excel

Summary

In this chapter, we have learned how to work with external storage, such as SD cards and microSD cards, on an ESP32 board. We also stored our sensor data into external storage. Lastly, we used a sensor monitoring logger by applying sleep mode after sensing and storing sensor data.

Next, we will learn how to communicate and interact with the internet on an ESP32 board.

5
Controlling IoT Devices over the Internet

Internet of Things (IoT) is one of the most popular topics in the technological industry. IoT can be applied in various scenarios, such as monitoring and automation. In this chapter, we will learn how to implement IoT on an ESP32 board through a Wi-Fi network. Here, we will begin to connect to an existing Wi-Fi and then make our own smart home application over Wi-Fi.

We will cover the following topics in this book:

- Connecting to an internet network via ESP32
- Accessing data from a web server
- Building a web server inside ESP32
- Making a smart home application

Technical requirements

Before we begin, make sure you have the following things ready:

- A computer with an OS installed, such as Windows, Linux, or macOS.
- An ESP32 development board. We recommend the ESP-WROVER-KIT v4 board from Espressif.
- A Wi-Fi network with internet access capability.

Introducing ESP32 Wi-Fi development

Wi-Fi, or a wireless network, is a communication model that makes it possible to interact with another system. With these, we can perform common network tasks over network protocols such as TCP/IP, UDP/IP, HTTP, or SMTP/POP3. Since the ESP32 chip has built-in Wi-Fi and a Bluetooth module, we connect our ESP32 board to an existing network.

To work with Wi-Fi on ESP32, we need the `esp_wifi.h` header file to be included in our project:

```
#include "esp_wifi.h"
```

Wi-Fi programming in ESP32 uses an event-based model. We call the Wi-Fi API from the board driver in order to access the Wi-Fi module on the ESP32 board. The ESP32 Wi-Fi API supports Wi-Fi security such as WPA, WPA2, and WEP. A list of Wi-Fi API functions can be found at https://docs.espressif.com/projects/esp-idf/en/latest/api-reference/network/esp_wifi.html.

In this chapter, we will work with a Wi-Fi network stack in the ESP32 board. For demo purposes, I have used the ESP-WROVER-KIT v4 board.

Scanning Wi-Fi hotspot

The first demo is used to perform Wi-Fi scanning. We will scan for all existing Wi-Fi networks in the surrounding area in which we are present. First, we will create the ESP32 project, called `wifiscan`. Our main program is `wifiscan.c`.

Next, we load all libraries from header files into our program as follows:

```
#include <string.h>
#include "freertos/FreeRTOS.h"
#include "freertos/task.h"
#include "freertos/event_groups.h"
#include "esp_system.h"
#include "esp_wifi.h"
#include "esp_event_loop.h"
#include "esp_log.h"
#include "nvs_flash.h"

#include "lwip/err.h"
#include "lwip/sys.h"
```

In the main `entry app_main()` function, we initialize storage for the Wi-Fi program by calling the `esp_wifi_set_storage()` function. We also need a function to listen to incoming events from the Wi-Fi API. For instance, we create a function named `event_handler()` and pass it into the `esp_event_loop_init()` function.

Next, we run the Wi-Fi service on ESP32 by calling the `esp_wifi_start()` function:

```
esp_err_t ret = nvs_flash_init();
if (ret == ESP_ERR_NVS_NO_FREE_PAGES || ret ==
ESP_ERR_NVS_NEW_VERSION_FOUND) {
    ESP_ERROR_CHECK(nvs_flash_erase());
    ret = nvs_flash_init();
}
ESP_ERROR_CHECK( ret );

tcpip_adapter_init();
ESP_ERROR_CHECK(esp_event_loop_init(event_handler, NULL));
wifi_init_config_t cfg = WIFI_INIT_CONFIG_DEFAULT();
ESP_ERROR_CHECK(esp_wifi_init(&cfg));
ESP_ERROR_CHECK(esp_wifi_set_storage(WIFI_STORAGE_RAM));
ESP_ERROR_CHECK(esp_wifi_set_mode(WIFI_MODE_STA));
ESP_ERROR_CHECK(esp_wifi_start());
```

After the Wi-Fi service has started, we will perform Wi-Fi scanning using the `esp_wifi_scan_start()` function. To do this, we should pass the `wifi_scan_config_t` parameter into `esp_wifi_scan_start()`. For Wi-Fi scanning, we set `NULL` for the `ssid` and `bssid` parameters.

We perform looping in Wi-Fi scanning. After the Wi-Fi scanning process is done, we again call `esp_wifi_scan_start()`:

```
wifi_scan_config_t scanConf = {
    .ssid = NULL,
    .bssid = NULL,
    .channel = 0,
    .show_hidden = true
};

while(true){
ESP_ERROR_CHECK(esp_wifi_scan_start(&scanConf, true));
vTaskDelay(3000 / portTICK_PERIOD_MS);
}
```

Now, we will implement the event_handler() function. Technically, we receive all events from the Wi-Fi service. You can read about Wi-Fi events in the ESP32 documentation at https://docs.espressif.com/projects/esp-idf/en/latest/api-guides/wifi.html.

In this scenario, we will wait for the SYSTEM_EVENT_SCAN_DONE event. This event is raised after ESP32 performs the Wi-Fi scanning. To get the result of Wi-Fi scanning, we can call the esp_wifi_scan_get_ap_num() function.

Then, we will loop our program to retrieve Wi-Fi hotspot information by calling the esp_wifi_scan_get_ap_records() function. We will then print the Wi-Fi information into the Terminal as follows:

```
esp_err_t event_handler(void *ctx, system_event_t *event)
{
    if (event->event_id == SYSTEM_EVENT_SCAN_DONE) {
        uint16_t apCount = 0;
        esp_wifi_scan_get_ap_num(&apCount);
        printf("Wi-Fi  found: %d\n",event->event_info.scan_done.number);
        if (apCount == 0) {
            return ESP_OK;
        }
        wifi_ap_record_t *wifi = (wifi_ap_record_t
*)malloc(sizeof(wifi_ap_record_t) * apCount);
        ESP_ERROR_CHECK(esp_wifi_scan_get_ap_records(&apCount, wifi));
....
}
```

After we have obtained a list of wifi_ap_record_t items, we will set the authentication name based on the wifi_ap_record_t.authmode type, as follows:

```
for (int i=0; i<apCount; i++) {
    char *authmode;
    switch(wifi[i].authmode) {
      case WIFI_AUTH_OPEN:
          authmode = "NO AUTH";
          break;
      case WIFI_AUTH_WEP:
          authmode = "WEP";
          break;
      case WIFI_AUTH_WPA_PSK:
          authmode = "WPA PSK";
          break;
      case WIFI_AUTH_WPA2_PSK:
          authmode = "WPA2 PSK";
          break;
      case WIFI_AUTH_WPA_WPA2_PSK:
          authmode = "WPA/WPA2 PSK";
```

```
        break;
    default:
        authmode = "Unknown";
        break;
}
```

Then, we will print Wi-Fi SSID, RSSI, and authentication mode onto the Terminal:

```
printf("SSID: %15.15s RSSI: %4d AUTH: %10.10s\n",wifi[i].ssid,
wifi[i].rssi, authmode);
```

Now you can save your project. Compile and flash this program into ESP32 board. I recommend using an 4 MB flash in your ESP32 board via the menuconfig application. Read Chapter 2, *Making Visual Data and Animation on an LCD,* and Chapter 3, *Building a Simple Game with an Embedded ESP32 Board,* to learn about configuring flash storage.

After a program is flashed on the screen, you can check the results of the Wi-Fi scanning using serial application. In figure 5-1, you can see that it shows the results of Wi-Fi scanning on my board:

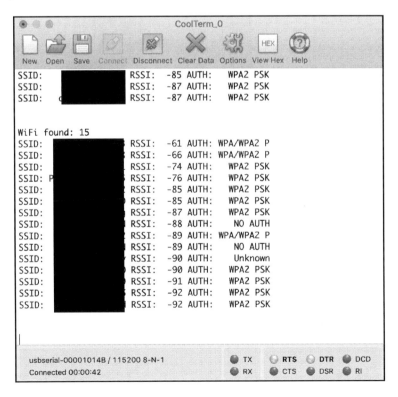

Figure 5-1: A result of Wi-Fi scanning

Connecting to an existing Wi-Fi network

In this section, we will be connecting to an existing Wi-Fi network. You should prepare a Wi-Fi hotspot for demo purposes. For Wi-Fi security, we will use WPA/WPA2 on an existing Wi-Fi network. Since we are using WPA/WPA2 authentication mode, we need the SSID name and SSID key from your Wi-Fi hotspot in order to join this Wi-Fi network.

We can now start to create a project called `wificonnect`. In the main entry, the `app_main()` function, we call the `connect_to_wifi()` function. The `connect_to_wifi()` function is the function that connects to existing Wi-Fi networks:

```
void app_main()
{
    //Initialize NVS
    esp_err_t ret = nvs_flash_init();
    if (ret == ESP_ERR_NVS_NO_FREE_PAGES || ret ==
ESP_ERR_NVS_NEW_VERSION_FOUND) {
        ESP_ERROR_CHECK(nvs_flash_erase());
        ret = nvs_flash_init();
    }
    ESP_ERROR_CHECK(ret);
    connect_to_wifi();
}
```

Technically, we initialize the Wi-Fi service in the `connect_to_wifi()` function. Since we want to connect to existing Wi-Fi, we should pass `SSID` and `SSID KEY` into the `wifi_config_t` parameter in the `esp_wifi_set_config()` function.

We will also pass the `event_handler()` function into the `esp_event_loop_init()` function to listen to all the events from a Wi-Fi service. We set our Wi-Fi service mode as `WIFI_MODE_STA` for the Wi-Fi station using the `esp_wifi_set_mode()` function. We will then start the Wi-Fi service by calling the `esp_wifi_start()` function.

We will then write the following program for the Wi-Fi service:

```
void connect_to_wifi()
{
    s_wifi_event_group = xEventGroupCreate();

    tcpip_adapter_init();
    ESP_ERROR_CHECK(esp_event_loop_init(event_handler, NULL) );

    wifi_init_config_t cfg = WIFI_INIT_CONFIG_DEFAULT();
    ESP_ERROR_CHECK(esp_wifi_init(&cfg));
    wifi_config_t wifi_config = {
```

```
            .sta = {
                .ssid = "SSID",
                .password = "SSID_KEY"
            },
        };

        ESP_ERROR_CHECK(esp_wifi_set_mode(WIFI_MODE_STA) );
        ESP_ERROR_CHECK(esp_wifi_set_config(ESP_IF_WIFI_STA, &wifi_config) );
        ESP_ERROR_CHECK(esp_wifi_start() );

        ESP_LOGI(TAG, "wifi_init_sta finished.");
    }
```

In the `event_handler()` function, we listen to three events: SYSTEM_EVENT_STA_START, SYSTEM_EVENT_STA_GOT_IP, and SYSTEM_EVENT_STA_DISCONNECTED. When we receive the SYSTEM_EVENT_STA_START event, we can call `esp_wifi_connect()` to connect to an existing Wi-Fi network.

We will get the SYSTEM_EVENT_STA_GOT_IP event if our ESP32 board gets an IP address from a Wi-Fi network. In this event, we print out our IP address for the ESP32 board:

```
static esp_err_t event_handler(void *ctx, system_event_t *event)
{
    switch(event->event_id) {
    case SYSTEM_EVENT_STA_START:
        esp_wifi_connect();
        break;
    case SYSTEM_EVENT_STA_GOT_IP:
        ESP_LOGI(TAG, "got ip:%s",
                    ip4addr_ntoa(&event->event_info.got_ip.ip_info.ip));
        s_retry_num = 0;
        xEventGroupSetBits(s_wifi_event_group, WIFI_CONNECTED_BIT);
        break;
```

The SYSTEM_EVENT_STA_DISCONNECTED event is used to detect whether or not our ESP32 board fails or disconnects from the Wi-Fi network. We call the `esp_wifi_connect()` function again to connect to an existing Wi-Fi network:

```
    case SYSTEM_EVENT_STA_DISCONNECTED:
        {
            if (s_retry_num < WIFI_ESP_MAXIMUM_RETRY) {
                esp_wifi_connect();
                xEventGroupClearBits(s_wifi_event_group,
WIFI_CONNECTED_BIT);
                s_retry_num++;
                ESP_LOGI(TAG,"retry to connect to the AP");
            }
```

```
                ESP_LOGI(TAG,"connect to the AP fail\n");
                break;
        }
    default:
        break;
    }
    return ESP_OK;
}
```

Save this project, and compile and flash the program onto the ESP32 board.

Figure 5-2 shows the program output when the ESP32 board is connected to a Wi-Fi hotspot:

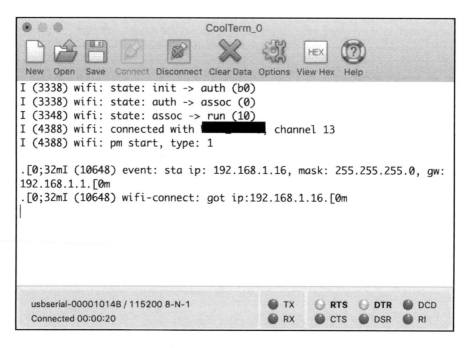

Figure 5-2: Getting IP address from existing Wi-Fi hotspot

Accessing data from a web server

In the previous section, we learned how to connect an existing Wi-Fi hotspot with an ESP32 board. Now, we will try to access a web server from our ESP32 board. Technically, ESP32 APIs adopt the socket programming model to communicate with other systems over a network.

For demo purposes, we will access a web server. We will use Google as a web server target here. We can start by creating the ESP32 project called `http_request`, with the `http_request.c` file as the main program. This project can also be found on the official website of the Espressif IDF project, at `https://github.com/espressif/esp-idf/tree/master/examples/protocols/http_server`.

1. First, we will load the libraries in our project, including the network libraries such as `socket.h` and `dns.h`:

```c
#include <string.h>
#include "freertos/FreeRTOS.h"
#include "freertos/task.h"
#include "freertos/event_groups.h"
#include "esp_system.h"
#include "esp_wifi.h"
#include "esp_event_loop.h"
#include "esp_log.h"
#include "nvs_flash.h"

#include "lwip/err.h"
#include "lwip/sockets.h"
#include "lwip/sys.h"
#include "lwip/netdb.h"
#include "lwip/dns.h"
```

2. We define our web server target as google.com. Since we use a socket programming model with the TCP/IP protocol, we should build our own HTTP request over the TCP/IP protocol. We will define the HTTP Get request on the REQUEST variable.

3. If you want to learn more about HTTP, I recommend reading the HTTP standard protocol in the RFC2616 document. You can read RFC 2616 at `https://tools.ietf.org/html/rfc2616`:

```c
#define WEB_SERVER "google.com"
#define WEB_PORT 80
#define WEB_URL "http://google.com/"

static const char *REQUEST = "GET " WEB_URL " HTTP/1.0\r\n"
    "Host: "WEB_SERVER"\r\n"
    "User-Agent: esp-idf/1.0 esp32\r\n"
    "\r\n";
```

4. To work with Wi-Fi on ESP32, we will start the Wi-Fi service on a main entry function called `app_main()`. We will also define our SSID and SSID key for our existing Wi-Fi. Change `SSID` and `SSID_KEY` from your Wi-Fi network configuration as follows:

```
wifi_config_t wifi_config = {
    .sta = {
        .ssid = "SSID",
        .password = "SSID_KEY",
    },
};
ESP_LOGI(TAG, "Setting Wi-Fi  configuration SSID %s...",
wifi_config.sta.ssid);
ESP_ERROR_CHECK( esp_wifi_set_mode(WIFI_MODE_STA) );
ESP_ERROR_CHECK( esp_wifi_set_config(ESP_IF_WIFI_STA, &wifi_config) );
ESP_ERROR_CHECK( esp_wifi_start() );
```

5. After we have connected to a Wi-Fi network, we will make an HTTP request to the web server. We will declare our socket with `SOCK_STREAM` for the TCP/IP protocol:

```
const struct addrinfo hints = {
    .ai_family = AF_INET,
    .ai_socktype = SOCK_STREAM,
};
struct addrinfo *res;
struct in_addr *addr;
int s, r;
char recv_buf[64];
```

6. Next, we will get the IP address from the web server using the `getaddrinfo()` function. Then, we will connect to the web server using the `connect()` function by passing the IP address of the web server target:

```
int err = getaddrinfo(WEB_SERVER, "80", &hints, &res);

if(err != 0 || res == NULL) {
    ESP_LOGE(TAG, "DNS lookup failed err=%d res=%p", err, res);
    vTaskDelay(1000 / portTICK_PERIOD_MS);
    continue;
}
addr = &((struct sockaddr_in *)res->ai_addr)->sin_addr;
ESP_LOGI(TAG, "DNS lookup succeeded. IP=%s", inet_ntoa(*addr));

s = socket(res->ai_family, res->ai_socktype, 0);
if(s < 0) {
    ESP_LOGE(TAG, "... Failed to allocate socket.");
```

```
        freeaddrinfo(res);
        vTaskDelay(1000 / portTICK_PERIOD_MS);
        continue;
    }
    ESP_LOGI(TAG, "... allocated socket");

    if(connect(s, res->ai_addr, res->ai_addrlen) != 0) {
        ESP_LOGE(TAG, "... socket connect failed errno=%d", errno);
        close(s);
        freeaddrinfo(res);
        vTaskDelay(4000 / portTICK_PERIOD_MS);
        continue;
    }

    ESP_LOGI(TAG, "... connected");
    freeaddrinfo(res);
```

7. After our ESP32 program is connected to the web server, we will make an HTTP GET request using the `write()` function by passing the REQUEST parameter that we defined in previous codes:

```
    if (write(s, REQUEST, strlen(REQUEST)) < 0) {
        ESP_LOGE(TAG, "... socket send failed");
        close(s);
        vTaskDelay(4000 / portTICK_PERIOD_MS);
        continue;
    }
    ESP_LOGI(TAG, "... socket send success");
```

8. Next, we will wait for an incoming response from the web server. We will set `timeout` for HTTP requests using `setsockopt()`. To read response messages from the web server, we can use the `read()` function. The response message from an web server is printed in the Terminal:

```
    struct timeval receiving_timeout;
    receiving_timeout.tv_sec = 5;
    receiving_timeout.tv_usec = 0;
    if (setsockopt(s, SOL_SOCKET, SO_RCVTIMEO, &receiving_timeout,
            sizeof(receiving_timeout)) < 0) {
        ESP_LOGE(TAG, "... failed to set socket receiving timeout");
        close(s);
        vTaskDelay(4000 / portTICK_PERIOD_MS);
        continue;
    }
    ESP_LOGI(TAG, "... set socket receiving timeout success");

    do {
```

```
        bzero(recv_buf, sizeof(recv_buf));
        r = read(s, recv_buf, sizeof(recv_buf)-1);
        for(int i = 0; i < r; i++) {
            putchar(recv_buf[i]);
        }
    } while(r > 0);
```

9. Once we've received all of the messages from the web server, we can close the connection using `close()`:

```
    close(s);
```

This program is applied with looping, so the program will connect and send a HTTP request to the web server continuously within a certain period. We can implement the looping delay with following code:

```
while(1) {
    ...

        for(int countdown = 10; countdown >= 0; countdown--) {
            ESP_LOGI(TAG, "%d... ", countdown);
            vTaskDelay(1000 / portTICK_PERIOD_MS);
        }
    ...
}
```

10. Save our project program, and compile and flash this program to the ESP32 board. Then you can use a serial app to see the program output:

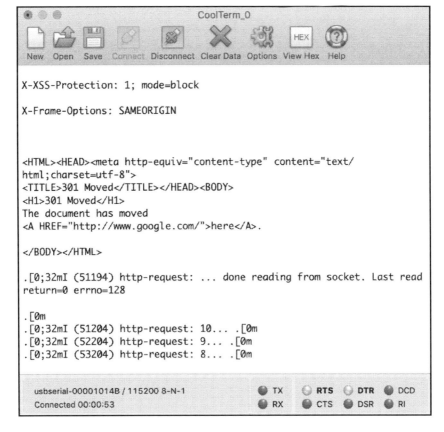

Figure 5-3: program output for the http_request project

Building your own web server inside ESP32

In this section, we will learn about a more advanced topic to build our own web server. A web server uses HTTP to serve all requests from clients. In this section, we will serve simple HTTP requests. We will use an existing sample program from the ESP32 web server project and implement the following three HTTP request scenarios:

- The HTTP `GET` request with the address `/hello`
- The HTTP `POST` request with the address `/echo`
- The HTTP `PUT` request with the address `/ctrl`

We will implement these requests in our web server.

Building HTTP requests

We will start our project by creating the ESP32 project, called **webserver**, with webserver.c as the main program. You can initialize the Wi-Fi service on the ESP32 that we have learned. For a web server with ESP32 API information, we can read the official document at https://docs.espressif.com/projects/esp-idf/en/latest/api-reference/protocols/esp_http_server.html.

To build a HTTP request, we will use the httpd_uri_t struct. We can declare the uri_get variable as the httpd_uri_t struct as follows:

```
httpd_uri_t uri_get = {
    .uri = "/uri",
    .method = HTTP_GET,
    .handler = get_handler,
    .user_ctx = NULL
};
```

httpd_uri_t.method can be HTTP_GET, HTTP_POST, and HTTP_PUT. We pass our function on httpd_uri_t.handler to process a HTTP request:

1. First, we will implement the /hello request. We will declare our HTTP GET request with the httpd_uri_t struct. Then, we will implement the HTTP GET handler function and create the hello_get_handler() function. We will then send the "Hello World!" message response to the client as follows:

```
httpd_uri_t hello = {
    .uri = "/hello",
    .method = HTTP_GET,
    .handler = hello_get_handler,
    /* Let's pass response string in user
     * context to demonstrate it's usage */
    .user_ctx = "Hello World!"
};
/* An HTTP GET handler */
esp_err_t hello_get_handler(httpd_req_t *req)
{
    char* buf;
    size_t buf_len;

    /* Get header value string length and allocate memory for length + 1,
     * extra byte for null termination */
    buf_len = httpd_req_get_hdr_value_len(req, "Host") + 1;
    if (buf_len > 1) {
        buf = malloc(buf_len);
        /* Copy null terminated value string into buffer */
```

```
            if (httpd_req_get_hdr_value_str(req, "Host", buf, buf_len) ==
ESP_OK) {
                ESP_LOGI(TAG, "Found header => Host: %s", buf);
            }
            free(buf);
        }

        buf_len = httpd_req_get_hdr_value_len(req, "Test-Header-2") + 1;
        if (buf_len > 1) {
            buf = malloc(buf_len);
            if (httpd_req_get_hdr_value_str(req, "Test-Header-2", buf, buf_len)
== ESP_OK) {
                ESP_LOGI(TAG, "Found header => Test-Header-2: %s", buf);
            }
            free(buf);
        }

        buf_len = httpd_req_get_hdr_value_len(req, "Test-Header-1") + 1;
        if (buf_len > 1) {
            buf = malloc(buf_len);
            if (httpd_req_get_hdr_value_str(req, "Test-Header-1", buf, buf_len)
== ESP_OK) {
                ESP_LOGI(TAG, "Found header => Test-Header-1: %s", buf);
            }
            free(buf);
        }
```

Read URL query string length and allocate memory for length + 1; extra byte for null termination.

```
    buf_len = httpd_req_get_url_query_len(req) + 1;
    if (buf_len > 1) {
    buf = malloc(buf_len);
    if (httpd_req_get_url_query_str(req, buf, buf_len) == ESP_OK) {
    ESP_LOGI(TAG, "Found URL query => %s", buf);
    char param[32];
    /* Get value of expected key from query string */
    if (httpd_query_key_value(buf, "query1", param, sizeof(param)) == ESP_OK)
    {
    ESP_LOGI(TAG, "Found URL query parameter => query1=%s", param);
    }
    if (httpd_query_key_value(buf, "query3", param, sizeof(param)) == ESP_OK)
    {
    ESP_LOGI(TAG, "Found URL query parameter => query3=%s", param);
    }
    if (httpd_query_key_value(buf, "query2", param, sizeof(param)) == ESP_OK)
    {
    ESP_LOGI(TAG, "Found URL query parameter => query2=%s", param);
```

```
    }
  }
  free(buf);
  }

  /* Set some custom headers */
```

Set some custom headers to the code:

```
  httpd_resp_set_hdr(req, "Custom-Header-1", "Custom-Value-1");
  httpd_resp_set_hdr(req, "Custom-Header-2", "Custom-Value-2");

  /* Send response with custom headers and body set as the
   * string passed in user context*/
  const char* resp_str = (const char*) req->user_ctx;
  httpd_resp_send(req, resp_str, strlen(resp_str));

  /* After sending the HTTP response the old HTTP request
   * headers are lost. Check if HTTP request headers can be read now. */
  if (httpd_req_get_hdr_value_len(req, "Host") == 0) {
  ESP_LOGI(TAG, "Request headers lost");
  }
  return ESP_OK;
  }
```

2. The second request is the `/echo` request. We declare our HTTP `POST` request with the `httpd_uri_t` struct. Then, we implement the HTTP `POST` handler function and create the `echo_post_header()` function. We implement an `echo` program. This program sends back content from the client. We can use the `httpd_resp_send_chunk()` function to send a content or request to a client:

```
httpd_uri_t echo = {
    .uri = "/echo",
    .method = HTTP_POST,
    .handler = echo_post_handler,
    .user_ctx = NULL
};
/* An HTTP POST handler */
esp_err_t echo_post_handler(httpd_req_t *req)
{
    char buf[100];
    int ret, remaining = req->content_len;

    while (remaining > 0) {
        /* Read the data for the request */
        if ((ret = httpd_req_recv(req, buf,
                    MIN(remaining, sizeof(buf)))) <= 0) {
```

```
                if (ret == HTTPD_SOCK_ERR_TIMEOUT) {
                    /* Retry receiving if timeout occurred */
                    continue;
                }
                return ESP_FAIL;
            }
            /* Send back the same data */
            httpd_resp_send_chunk(req, buf, ret);
            remaining -= ret;
            /* Log data received */
            ESP_LOGI(TAG, "=========== RECEIVED DATA ==========");
            ESP_LOGI(TAG, "%.*s", ret, buf);
            ESP_LOGI(TAG, "====================================");
        }
        // End response
        httpd_resp_send_chunk(req, NULL, 0);
        return ESP_OK;
    }
```

3. The last request is the /ctrl request. This request implements HTTP PUT. Our aim is to register and unregister based on user input. When the user sends 1, we register the /hello and /echo HTTP requests. If not, we unregister all requests when we receive a value of 0:

```
httpd_uri_t ctrl = {
    .uri = "/ctrl",
    .method = HTTP_PUT,
    .handler = ctrl_put_handler,
    .user_ctx = NULL
};

/* An HTTP PUT handler. This demonstrates realtime
 * registration and deregistration of URI handlers
 */
esp_err_t ctrl_put_handler(httpd_req_t *req)
{
    char buf;
    int ret;

    if ((ret = httpd_req_recv(req, &buf, 1)) <= 0) {
        if (ret == HTTPD_SOCK_ERR_TIMEOUT) {
            httpd_resp_send_408(req);
        }
        return ESP_FAIL;
    }

    if (buf == '0') {
```

```
        /* Handler can be unregistered using the uri string */
        ESP_LOGI(TAG, "Unregistering /hello and /echo URIs");
        httpd_unregister_uri(req->handle, "/hello");
        httpd_unregister_uri(req->handle, "/echo");
    }
    else {
        ESP_LOGI(TAG, "Registering /hello and /echo URIs");
        httpd_register_uri_handler(req->handle, &hello);
        httpd_register_uri_handler(req->handle, &echo);
    }

    /* Respond with empty body */
    httpd_resp_send(req, NULL, 0);
    return ESP_OK;
}
```

Next, we will write our web server.

Building a web server

In this section, we will activate our web server on the ESP32 board. When we receive a SYSTEM_EVENT_STA_GOT_IP event from Wi-Fi service, we start a web server by calling the start_webserver() function.

1. We will call the stop_webserver() function when the ESP32 board is disconnected on a SYSTEM_EVENT_STA_DISCONNECTED event:

```
static esp_err_t event_handler(void *ctx, system_event_t *event)
{
    httpd_handle_t *server = (httpd_handle_t *) ctx;

    switch(event->event_id) {
    case SYSTEM_EVENT_STA_START:
        ESP_LOGI(TAG, "SYSTEM_EVENT_STA_START");
        ESP_ERROR_CHECK(esp_wifi_connect());
        break;
    case SYSTEM_EVENT_STA_GOT_IP:
        ESP_LOGI(TAG, "SYSTEM_EVENT_STA_GOT_IP");
        ESP_LOGI(TAG, "Got IP: '%s'",
                ip4addr_ntoa(&event->event_info.got_ip.ip_info.ip));

        /* Start the web server */
        if (*server == NULL) {
            *server = start_webserver();
        }
        break;
```

```
    case SYSTEM_EVENT_STA_DISCONNECTED:
        ESP_LOGI(TAG, "SYSTEM_EVENT_STA_DISCONNECTED");
        ESP_ERROR_CHECK(esp_wifi_connect());

        /* Stop the web server */
        if (*server) {
            stop_webserver(*server);
            *server = NULL;
        }
        break;
    default:
        break;
    }
    return ESP_OK;
}
```

2. Now, we will implement the start_webserver() function. We will first use
   httpd_start() to start our web server. Then, we will register all HTTP requests
   using the httpd_register_uri_handler() function:

```
httpd_handle_t start_webserver(void)
{
    httpd_handle_t server = NULL;
    httpd_config_t config = HTTPD_DEFAULT_CONFIG();

    // Start the httpd server
    ESP_LOGI(TAG, "Starting server on port: '%d'", config.server_port);
    if (httpd_start(&server, &config) == ESP_OK) {
        // Set URI handlers
        ESP_LOGI(TAG, "Registering URI handlers");
        httpd_register_uri_handler(server, &hello);
        httpd_register_uri_handler(server, &echo);
        httpd_register_uri_handler(server, &ctrl);
        return server;
    }

    ESP_LOGI(TAG, "Error starting server!");
    return NULL;
}
```

3. To stop the web server service from working, we will implement the `stop_webserver()` function. We will also call the `httpd_stop()` function to stop our web server service in ESP32:

```
void stop_webserver(httpd_handle_t server)
{
    // Stop the httpd server
    httpd_stop(server);
}
```

4. Save all the programs.

Testing the program

Now you can compile and upload our project program into the ESP32 board. Open your serial app in order to see your IP Address. Figure 5-4 shows that our program has started. You should see your IP Address in the ESP32 board:

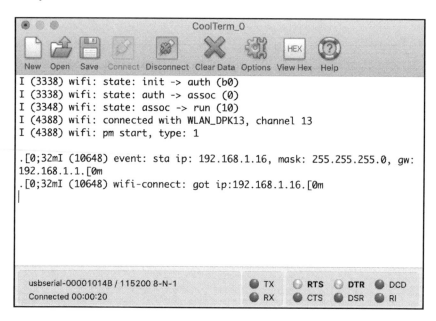

Figure 5-4: IP Address from the web server on the ESP32 board

Now you can use a browser for testing. Open the `http://<ip address of ESP32>/hello` URL. If this is successful, you will see the response message `"Hello World!"`, as shown in Figure 5-5:

Figure 5-5: A response output from ESP32 in the browser

To simulate a HTTP POST request, you can use the Postman program. You can download this at `https://www.getpostman.com/`.

Another option for the HTTP tools is to write a program to perform an HTTP POST request when we use the Postman tool. The Postman tool can be used to send a HTTP request with the GET, POST, DEL, and PUT modes. You can select POST with the `http://<ip address of ESP32>/echo` target URL:

```
Content-Type: application/x-www-form-urlencoded
```

We set the request body as a `hello world` message. You can see the HTTP POST request on Postman in figure 5-6:

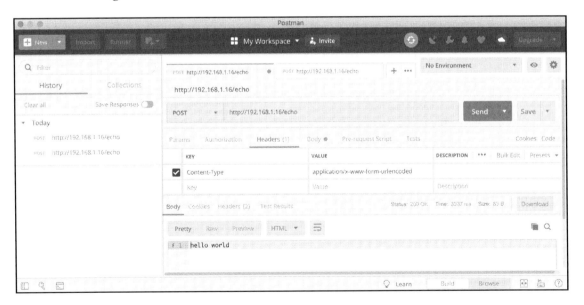

Figure 5-6: Performing HTTP POST request using Postman

Click the **Send** button to execute the HTTP POST request. You should get a response from ESP32 with the requested message. The request body should have similar content to your Postman tool. You also can see program output in the ESP32 Terminal, as shown in figure 5-7:

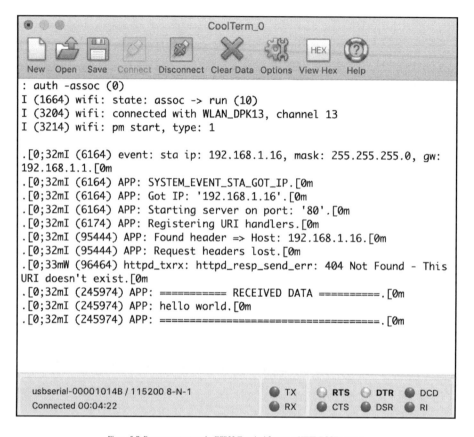

Figure 5-7: Program output on the ESP32 Terminal from our HTTP POST request

For the HTTP PUT request, we can use the same configuration from the HTTP POST request. We will set PUT on the Postman tool. On the body request, we will then set the value as 1 or 0. If we set it as 1, the ESP32 program will register the /hello and /echo requests. Otherwise, we will set the value as 0 to unregister all requests. You can see my Postman configuration in figure 5-8:

Figure 5-8: Performing an HTTP PUT request using Postman

Press the **Send** button to execute the HTTP PUT request. You can see the program output on the ESP32 Terminal in figure 5-9:

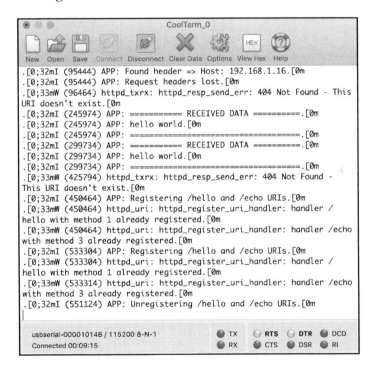

Figure 5-9: Program output on the ESP32 Terminal from our HTTP PUT request

Try to change the request body with a value of 0. Then press the **Send** button in the Postman tool.

Project - making a smart home

In this project, we will build a simple smart home application. A smart home application is an application based on technology that enables users to control devices within the house. This application is connected to some sensors and devices. We can get information about our home through sensor devices such as cameras, temperature, and electricity usage. We can also control turning lamps on and off.

In this section, we will build a simple smart home using ESP32. We can see a general design of smart home with the ESP32 board in the following diagram. We can connect sensor and actuator devices to the ESP32 board, and we can then control them over the network.

To enable us to control the ESP32 board from outside the house, we should activate a web server service. We define our commands to ESP32 through the web server, as explained in the following diagram:

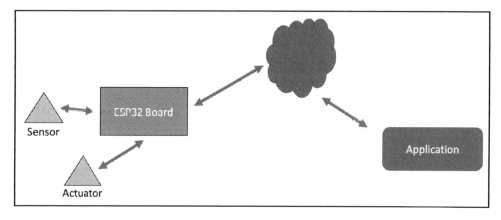

Figure 5-10: A simple model of a smart home application

For a simple demo, we use an LED in an ESP32 board. We will turn this LED on/off via HTTP requests. We will define the /led HTTP request to turn the LED on and off. If a program receives a value of 1 in a request body, we turn on the LED; otherwise, we, turn off the LED when the program receives a value of 0.

Next, we will implement our project.

Hardware wiring

Hardware wiring does not require much effort; we only need one LED that is connected to IO12 pin of the ESP32 board. You can change the IO12 pin if your ESP32 board does not expose this GPIO pin.

Handling HTTP requests

Now we will develop a program for our smart home project:

1. Create a project called smarthome. Our main program is the smarthome.c file.

First, we will declare our libraries for this project:

```
#include <esp_wifi.h>
#include <esp_event_loop.h>
#include <esp_log.h>
#include <esp_system.h>
#include <nvs_flash.h>
#include <sys/param.h>

#include <esp_http_server.h>
```

2. We will then define our logger title and GPIO for our LED:

```
static const char *TAG="APP";
#define LED1 12
```

3. Next, we will develop a HTTP POST request handler via the `httpd_uri_t` struct. We define the `/led` request with `HTTP_POST` for the request method. In addition, we pass the `led_post_handle()` function into the request handler as follows:

```
httpd_uri_t led_post = {
    .uri = "/led",
    .method = HTTP_POST,
    .handler = led_post_handler,
    .user_ctx = NULL
};
```

4. Now we implement our `led_post_handler()` function. This function reads the HTTP request message. Then, check whether the request body has a value of 1 or 0 in the HTTP request body. If the request body consists of value 1, we turn on the LED by calling the `gpio_set_level()` function:

```
esp_err_t led_post_handler(httpd_req_t *req)
{
    char buf[100];
    int ret, remaining = req->content_len;

    while (remaining > 0) {
        buf[0] = '\0';
        if ((ret = httpd_req_recv(req, &buf, 1)) <= 0) {
            if (ret == HTTPD_SOCK_ERR_TIMEOUT) {
                httpd_resp_send_408(req);
            }
            return ESP_FAIL;
        }
        buf[ret] = '\0';
        ESP_LOGI(TAG, "Recv HTTP => %s", buf);
        if (buf[0] == '1') {
            ESP_LOGI(TAG, "=====================================");
            ESP_LOGI(TAG, ">>> Turn on LED");
            gpio_set_level(LED1, 1);
            httpd_resp_send_chunk(req, "Turn on LED", ret);
        }
        else
        if (buf[0] == '0') {
            ESP_LOGI(TAG, "=====================================");
            ESP_LOGI(TAG, ">>> Turn off LED");
            gpio_set_level(LED1, 0);
            httpd_resp_send_chunk(req, "Turn off LED", ret);
        }
        else {
            ESP_LOGI(TAG, "=====================================");
            ESP_LOGI(TAG, ">>> Unknow command");
```

```
            httpd_resp_send_chunk(req, "Unknow command", ret);
        }
        remaining -= ret;
    }

    // End response
    httpd_resp_send_chunk(req, NULL, 0);
    return ESP_OK;
}
```

5. Next, we will develop a web server in the ESP32 board.

Writing a web server program

In this section, we will implement the web server that we learned about in the previous section in this chapter:

1. We will call the `initialize_gpio()` and `initialize_wifi()` functions to initialize GPIO and Wi-Fi as follows:

```
void app_main()
{
    static httpd_handle_t server = NULL;
    ESP_ERROR_CHECK(nvs_flash_init());
    initialize_gpio();
    initialize_wifi(&server);
}
```

2. We will set GPIO to output mode on the `initialize_gpio()` function, as follows:

```
static void initialize_gpio(){
    // set gpio and its direction
    gpio_pad_select_gpio(LED1);
    gpio_set_direction(LED1, GPIO_MODE_OUTPUT);
}
```

3. In the `initialize_wifi()` function, we will initialize our Wi-Fi service. You should set `SSID` and `SSID_KEY` in order to connect to an existing Wi-Fi network:

```
static void initialize_wifi(void *arg)
{
    tcpip_adapter_init();
    ESP_ERROR_CHECK(esp_event_loop_init(event_handler, arg));
    wifi_init_config_t cfg = WIFI_INIT_CONFIG_DEFAULT();
    ESP_ERROR_CHECK(esp_wifi_init(&cfg));
    ESP_ERROR_CHECK(esp_wifi_set_storage(WIFI_STORAGE_RAM));
    wifi_config_t wifi_config = {
        .sta = {
            .ssid = "SSID",
            .password = "SSID_KEY",
        },
    };
    ESP_LOGI(TAG, "Setting Wi-Fi  configuration SSID %s...",
wifi_config.sta.ssid);
    ESP_ERROR_CHECK(esp_wifi_set_mode(WIFI_MODE_STA));
    ESP_ERROR_CHECK(esp_wifi_set_config(ESP_IF_WIFI_STA, &wifi_config));
    ESP_ERROR_CHECK(esp_wifi_start());
}
```

4. We will define the `event_handler()` function to listen to events from a Wi-Fi service. After we receive an IP Address via the `SYSTEM_EVENT_STA_GOT_IP` event, we will run our web server by calling the `start_webserver()` function.

If we receive a `SYSTEM_EVENT_STA_DISCONNECTED` event, our program will disconnect from the Wi-Fi. Next, we should reconnect to the existing Wi-Fi network and stop our web server by calling the `stop_webserver()` function:

```
static esp_err_t event_handler(void *ctx, system_event_t *event)
{
    httpd_handle_t *server = (httpd_handle_t *) ctx;

    switch(event->event_id) {
    case SYSTEM_EVENT_STA_START:
        ESP_LOGI(TAG, "SYSTEM_EVENT_STA_START");
        ESP_ERROR_CHECK(esp_wifi_connect());
        break;
    case SYSTEM_EVENT_STA_GOT_IP:
        ESP_LOGI(TAG, "SYSTEM_EVENT_STA_GOT_IP");
        ESP_LOGI(TAG, "Got IP: '%s'",
                ip4addr_ntoa(&event->event_info.got_ip.ip_info.ip));

        /* Start the web server */
        if (*server == NULL) {
```

```
                *server = start_webserver();
        }
        break;
    case SYSTEM_EVENT_STA_DISCONNECTED:
        ESP_LOGI(TAG, "SYSTEM_EVENT_STA_DISCONNECTED");
        ESP_ERROR_CHECK(esp_wifi_connect());

        /* Stop the web server */
        if (*server) {
            stop_webserver(*server);
            *server = NULL;
        }
        break;
    default:
        break;
    }
    return ESP_OK;
}
```

5. We use the same codes from the `webserver` project to start and stop our web server. The following is the code implementation for the `start_webserver()` and `stop_webserver()` functions:

```
httpd_handle_t start_webserver(void)
{
    httpd_handle_t server = NULL;
    httpd_config_t config = HTTPD_DEFAULT_CONFIG();

    // Start the httpd server
    ESP_LOGI(TAG, "Starting server on port: '%d'", config.server_port);
    if (httpd_start(&server, &config) == ESP_OK) {
        // Set URI handlers
        ESP_LOGI(TAG, "Registering URI handlers");
        httpd_register_uri_handler(server, &led_post);
        return server;
    }

    ESP_LOGI(TAG, "Error starting server!");
    return NULL;
}

void stop_webserver(httpd_handle_t server)
{
    // Stop the httpd server
    httpd_stop(server);
}
```

6. Save all codes. Next, we can test our program.

Testing the program

You can compile and upload this project program onto the ESP32 board. Open the serial tool to navigate to your ESP32. You should see the IP address of the ESP32 board here. If you don't see it, please reset your board. Figure 5-11 shows the IP address of my ESP32 board:

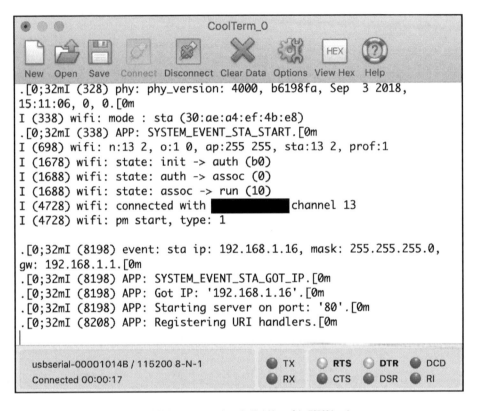

Figure 5-11: Program output shows the IP Address of the ESP32 board

For testing, we will use the Postman tool.

1. You can set the HTTP POST request with the following header:

```
Content-Type: application/x-www-form-urlencoded
```

2. Select the **raw** option for the request body in the Postman tool. Then, give a value of 1 to the body content, as shown in figure 5-12:

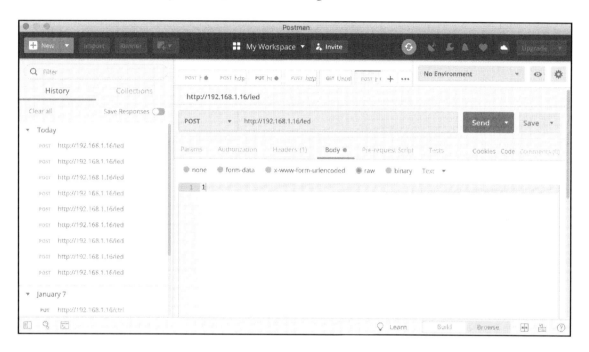

Figure 5-12: Sending HTTP requests using the Postman tool

3. Click the **Send** button to execute the HTTP POST request. You can see the ESP32 program output on the serial application, as shown in figure 5-13. Your LED should light up after receiving a value of 1 from the Postman tool:

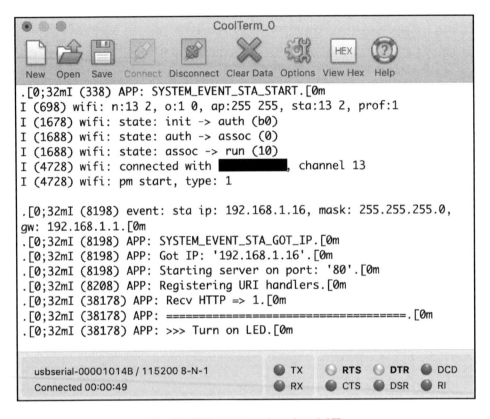

Figure 5-13: ESP32 program output when turning on the LED

4. Now you can change the value request, so instead of 1, we input a value of 0 in the Postman tool (see step 2). After doing this, click **Send**. You should see that your LED turns off at this point. Figure 5-14 shows the program output from ESP32:

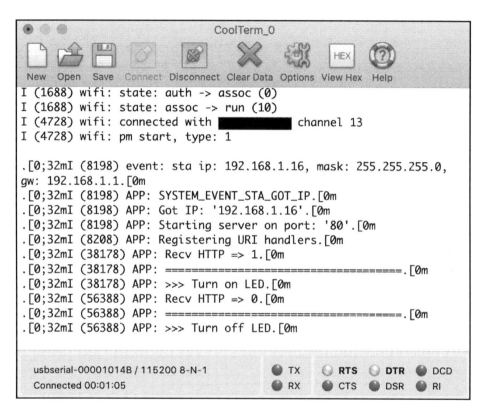

Figure 5-14: ESP32 program output when turning off the LED

5. Finally, you can send any message, except the 1 and 0 values, via the Postman tool. You should see that the ESP32 program shows an unknown command message, as shown in figure 5-15:

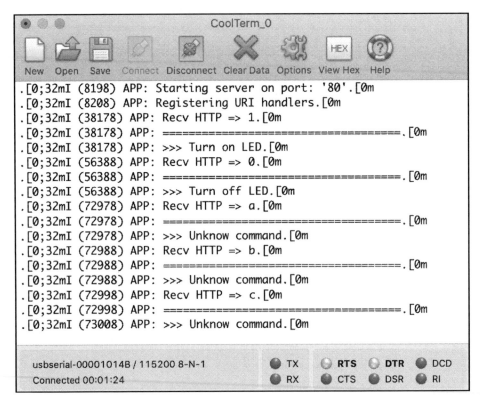

Figure 5-15: ESP32 program output when HTTP requests are not 1 or 0

This is the end of the chapter. You can practice further by adding command requests with some sensor and actuator devices.

Summary

First, we learned how to work with Wi-Fi on the ESP32 board. Then, our ESP32 board was connected to the internet and was accessed over a web server. We also made a simple web server on the ESP32 board. Finally, we built a simple smart home app by controlling an LED over a network.

Next, we will build a weather station system based on IoT with the ESP32 board.

Building an IoT Weather Station

In this chapter, we will continue to develop our understanding of how to build an **Internet of Things (IoT)**-based weather monitoring system, which we looked at in `Chapter 2`, *Making Visual Data and Animation on an LCD*. We will learn more practices to develop a weather monitoring system by adding internet connectivity capabilities. Furthermore, we will also learn how to handle requests from clients who are trying to access the service.

In this chapter, we will explore the following topics:

- Introducing a weather station
- Building an IoT weather station
- Handling large data requests for weather monitoring systems

Technical requirements

Before we begin, make sure you have the following things ready:

- A computer with an OS such as Windows, Linux, or macOS installed
- An ESP32 development board; the ESP-WROVER-KIT v4 board from Espressif is recommended
- A DHT22 module
- A Wi-Fi network with internet access capability

Introducing a weather station

In `Chapter 2`, *Making Visual Data and Animation on an LCD*, we learned what a weather monitoring system is. To build a weather station, we require an understanding of weather monitoring systems. We will focus on building a weather station in this chapter. A weather station has more features than a weather monitoring system; we can send a result of the measurement to the backend server on a weather station. In general, we can describe a simple model of a weather station-based IoT as shown in *Figure 6.1*. A weather station consists of the following modules:

- An **MCU** is used to process all computations.
- **Environmental sensors** are sensor devices used to convert physical objects into digital form. In the context of weather stations, environmental sensors can be temperature, humidity, wind speed, and direction.
- **A network module** is used to transfer sensor data to a server or a gateway. Data is then distributed to other systems.

The following figure shows a simple model of a weather station:

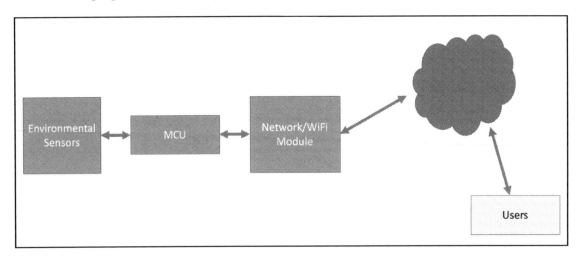

Figure 6.1: A simple model of a weather station

In this chapter, we explore how to develop a simple weather station with the ESP32 board. For this, we use the DHT module as an environmental sensor. We will use cloud-based technology in this model.

Working with DHT sensors

To build a weather station, we need environmental sensors. In Chapter 2, *Making Visual Data and Animation on an LCD*, we learned how to retrieve temperature and humidity from a DHT22 module, and displayed this in the LCD.

To work with DHT22, we declare a DHT module type and its GPIO pin on ESP32:

```
#include <dht.h>
static const dht_sensor_type_t sensor_type = DHT_TYPE_DHT22;
static const gpio_num_t dht_gpio = 26;
```

We can obtain the temperature and humidity from DHT22, and we can call the dht_read_data() function by passing temperature and humidity variables, as follows:

```
int16_t temperature = 0;
int16_t humidity = 0;

dht_read_data(sensor_type, dht_gpio, &humidity, &temperature);
```

Next, we will implement a weather station with ESP32.

Building an IoT weather station

In this section, we will build an IoT weather station with an ESP32 board and a DHT22 module. We build a web server inside ESP32 and create a /weather HTTP request to serve temperature and humidity. The scenario for our project is as follows:

- The user can access a weather station via a browser application request to http://<esp32_server>/weather.
- The ESP32 program serves a /weather request.
- The ESP32 program reads the temperature and humidity from the DHT22 module.
- The ESP32 program sends a response by sending HTML with the temperature and humidity data.

You can see our simple architecture in the following figure:

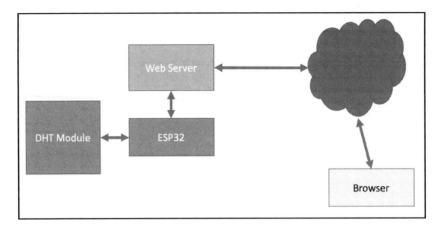

Figure 6.2: Implementing the weather station with ESP32

We will test our weather system using a browser. We need an existing Wi-Fi network to enable the ESP32 board and serve weather information.

So, let's start.

Hardware wiring

We use the same hardware wiring that we used in Chapter 2, *Making Visual Data and Animation on an LCD*, for a weather project. Our DHT22 module is connected to IO26 from the ESP32 board.

Writing the program

We start by creating a project called weatherweb to implement our program. Our main program file is weatherweb.c inside the main folder, which we will use to write this program on the weatherweb.c file:

1. Initialize all the required headers, as follows:

```
#include <esp_wifi.h>
#include <esp_event_loop.h>
#include <esp_log.h>
#include <esp_system.h>
#include <nvs_flash.h>
```

```
#include <sys/param.h>
#include <esp_http_server.h>
```

2. Define the DHT module as DHT22 and GPIO for the DHT module on the 26 pin:

```
#include <dht.h>
static const dht_sensor_type_t sensor_type = DHT_TYPE_DHT22;
static const gpio_num_t dht_gpio = 26;
```

3. Prepare our HTML response on the WEATHER_TXT variable:

```
static const char *TAG="APP";
static const char *WEATHER_TXT =
"<html>"
"<head><title>%s</title></head>"
"<body>"
"<p>Temperature: %d </p>"
"<p>Humidity: %d %%</p>"
"</body>"
"</html>";
```

You can see that the WEATHER_TXT variable consists of %s and %d. These parameters will be inserted along with a header title for the parameters listed in the preceding code. This includes the temperature, response, and humidity from our ESP32 program.

4. Now let's define the entry main program on the app_main() function. Define a web server variable called http_handle_t, and then initialize the Wi-Fi service by calling initialize_wifi() with a passing server variable:

```
void app_main()
{
    static httpd_handle_t server = NULL;
    ESP_ERROR_CHECK(nvs_flash_init());
    initialize_wifi(&server);
}
```

5. Implement the initialize_wifi() function to connect to an existing Wi-Fi and start a Wi-Fi service. You should change SSID and SSID_KEY for your existing Wi-Fi. Pass the event_handle() function to the esp_event_loop_init() function to listen to events from the Wi-Fi service:

```
static void initialize_wifi(void *arg)
{
    tcpip_adapter_init();
    ESP_ERROR_CHECK(esp_event_loop_init(event_handler, arg));
    wifi_init_config_t cfg = WIFI_INIT_CONFIG_DEFAULT();
    ESP_ERROR_CHECK(esp_wifi_init(&cfg));
```

```
    ESP_ERROR_CHECK(esp_wifi_set_storage(WIFI_STORAGE_RAM));
    wifi_config_t wifi_config = {
        .sta = {
            .ssid = "SSID",
            .password = "SSID_KEY",
        },
    };
```

We set the ESP32 Wi-Fi mode as `WIFI_MODE_STA` using `esp_wifi_mode()`. All Wi-Fi configs are passed to the `esp_wifi_set_config()` function to be executed by the ESP32 Wi-Fi service. To start the Wi-Fi service, we call the `esp_wifi_start()` function:

```
    ESP_LOGI(TAG, "Setting Wi-Fi configuration SSID %s...",
  wifi_config.sta.ssid);
    ESP_ERROR_CHECK(esp_wifi_set_mode(WIFI_MODE_STA));
    ESP_ERROR_CHECK(esp_wifi_set_config(ESP_IF_WIFI_STA, &wifi_config));
    ESP_ERROR_CHECK(esp_wifi_start());
}
```

In the `event_handler()` function, we listen to the following events: SYSTEM_EVENT_STA_START, SYSTEM_EVENT_STA_GOT_IP, and SYSTEM_EVENT_STA_DISCONNECTED. Then, we will perform the following steps to handle the incoming events:

1. Connect to the existing Wi-Fi by calling `esp_wifi_connect()` when we receive the SYSTEM_EVENT_STA_START event:

```
static esp_err_t event_handler(void *ctx, system_event_t *event)
{
    httpd_handle_t *server = (httpd_handle_t *) ctx;

    switch(event->event_id) {
    case SYSTEM_EVENT_STA_START:
        ESP_LOGI(TAG, "SYSTEM_EVENT_STA_START");
        ESP_ERROR_CHECK(esp_wifi_connect());
        break;
```

2. Start the web server by calling `start_webserver()` when we receive the SYSTEM_EVENT_STA_GOT_IP event:

```
    case SYSTEM_EVENT_STA_GOT_IP:
        ESP_LOGI(TAG, "SYSTEM_EVENT_STA_GOT_IP");
        ESP_LOGI(TAG, "Got IP: '%s'",
                ip4addr_ntoa(&event->event_info.got_ip.ip_info.ip));

        /* Start the web server */
        if (*server == NULL) {
```

```
        *server = start_webserver();
    }
    break;
```

3. Stop a web server by calling `stop_webserver()` when we receive the `SYSTEM_EVENT_STA_DISCONNECTED` event.

4. Reconnect to the existing Wi-Fi by calling the `esp_wifi_connect()` function:

```
case SYSTEM_EVENT_STA_DISCONNECTED:
        ESP_LOGI(TAG, "SYSTEM_EVENT_STA_DISCONNECTED");
        ESP_ERROR_CHECK(esp_wifi_connect());

        /* Stop the web server */
        if (*server) {
            stop_webserver(*server);
            *server = NULL;
        }
        break;
```

5. Next, implement the `start_webserver()` and `stop_webserver()` functions. On starting a web server, register our /weather HTTP request using the `httpd_register_uri_handler()` function by passing the `weather` variable. When our program receives the /weather HTTP request, we will call our function in the `weather` variable. We can stop our web server by calling `httpd_stop()`:

```
httpd_handle_t start_webserver(void)
{
    httpd_handle_t server = NULL;
    httpd_config_t config = HTTPD_DEFAULT_CONFIG();

    // Start the httpd server
    ESP_LOGI(TAG, "Starting server on port: '%d'", config.server_port);
    if (httpd_start(&server, &config) == ESP_OK) {
        // Set URI handlers
        ESP_LOGI(TAG, "Registering URI handlers");
        httpd_register_uri_handler(server, &weather);
        return server;
    }

    ESP_LOGI(TAG, "Error starting server!");
    return NULL;
}
```

6. The `stop_webserver()` function is used to stop the web server service. To stop our web server, we can call `httpd_stop()`:

```
void stop_webserver(httpd_handle_t server)
{
    // Stop the httpd server
    httpd_stop(server);
}
```

7. Define a `weather` variable with `httpd_uri_t`. Then, declare our `/weather` HTTP request on `uri`. After doing this, we pass the `weather_get_handler()` function to the handler, as follows:

```
httpd_uri_t weather = {
    .uri = "/weather",
    .method = HTTP_GET,
    .handler = weather_get_handler,
    .user_ctx = "ESP32 Weather System"
};
```

8. Implement the `weather_get_handler()` function to read the temperature and humidity from the `DHT22` module using the `dht_read_data()` function:

```
esp_err_t weather_get_handler(httpd_req_t *req)
{
    ESP_LOGI(TAG, "Request headers lost");
    int16_t temperature = 0;
    int16_t humidity = 0;
    char tmp_buff[256];

    if (dht_read_data(sensor_type, dht_gpio, &humidity, &temperature) ==
ESP_OK)
    {
        sprintf(tmp_buff, WEATHER_TXT, (const char*) req->user_ctx,
temperature/10, humidity/10);
    }
```

9. Then, send a response message with the `httpd_resp_send()` function, as follows:

```
httpd_resp_send(req, tmp_buff, strlen(tmp_buff));

if (httpd_req_get_hdr_value_len(req, "Host") == 0) {
    ESP_LOGI(TAG, "Request headers lost");
}
```

After saving all the code, let's test our program.

Testing the program

We've just written our program, `weatherweb`, so it's time to compile and upload it to the ESP32 board; you can type this command:

```
$ make flash
```

Now we can test our program. To do this, open a serial software, such as CoolTerm, to connect to the ESP32 board. You should see that your ESP32 board gets an IP address from the Wi-Fi hotspot, as shown in the following figure:

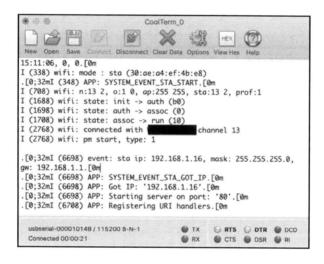

Figure 6.3: The ESP32 program output on the serial Terminal

For instance, if the IP address for the ESP32 board is `192.168.1.16`, you can open a browser and navigate to `http://192.168.1.16/weather`. You should get the temperature and humidity data from the ESP32 board; *Figure 6.4* shows a sample output:

Figure 6.4: A browser feeding sensor data from ESP32

We've now set up a basic program that provides us with temperature and humidity data when queried. Next, we are going to make our program perform an auto-refresh with the weather application.

The auto-refresh weather application

We will now set up a weatherweb project. Here, we will receive information about temperature and humidity via a browser. If you want to get the latest information from the ESP32 board, you will have to open a new request to the ESP32 board manually. Let's now automate this activity, as follows:

1. To perform an auto-refresh on HTML, use http-equiv="refresh" on the <meta> tag. We can modify our weatherweb project by declaring the WEATHER_TXT_REF variable:

```
static const char *WEATHER_TXT_REF =
"<html>"
"<head><title>%s</title>"
"<meta http-equiv=\"refresh\" content=\"5\" >"
"</head>"
"<body>"
"<p>Temperature: %d </p>"
"<p>Humidity: %d %%</p>"
"</body>"
"</html>";
```

2. On the weather_get handler() function, change WEATHER_TXT to WEATHER_TXT_REF on the sprintf() function:

```
esp_err_t weather_get_handler(httpd_req_t *req)
{
    ESP_LOGI(TAG, "Request headers lost");
    int16_t temperature = 0;
    int16_t humidity = 0;
    char tmp_buff[256];

    if (dht_read_data(sensor_type, dht_gpio, &humidity, &temperature) ==
ESP_OK)
    {
        sprintf(tmp_buff, WEATHER_TXT_REF, (const char*) req->user_ctx,
temperature/10, humidity/10);
    }else{
        tmp_buff[0]='\0';
    }
```

Then, we send data to the client by calling the `http_resp_send()` function:

```
httpd_resp_send(req, tmp_buff, strlen(tmp_buff));

if (httpd_req_get_hdr_value_len(req, "Host") == 0) {
    ESP_LOGI(TAG, "Request headers lost");
}
return ESP_OK;
}
```

3. Save this code, and then try to compile and upload this program into the ESP32 board.
4. Now we can test our program; open a browser and navigate to `http://<ip address of ESP32 board>/weather`. You should get a web form, as shown in the preceding section. This browser output will auto-refresh every five seconds.

Now that we've set up the weather station and configured it to give an auto-refreshed output every five seconds, let's move on to dealing with scalability.

Handling a massive data request for a weather station

An ESP32 board has limited resources. We can push an ESP32 board to handle massive requests from clients. To serve large requests from clients, we can use a production web server. A production web server will make a request from the ESP32 board, and then broadcast to all the requesters or clients.

We can draw our general design for the ESP32 board to address massive requests in *Figure 6.5*. We can use Node.js as the web server to serve requests from clients. We also use `Socket.io` to broadcast messages to all requesters. `Socket.io` uses WebSocket technology to enable us to work with a full-duplex TCP connection on a browser.

You can learn about `Socket.io` at `https://socket.io/`:

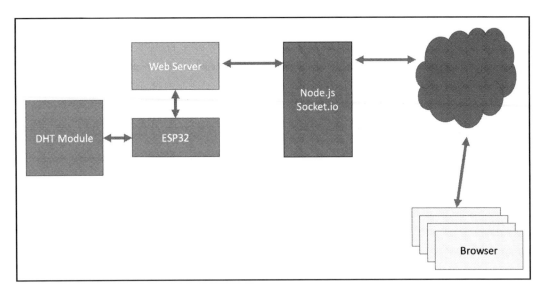

Figure 6.5: Applying the Node.js server as a backend system

In this section, we'll develop a program with Node.js and Socket.io to serve all requests for the sensor from the ESP32 board. Node.js will visualize the temperature data from the ESP32 board.

In the next section, we will develop a program for the ESP32 board.

Writing a program for ESP32

We do not need to create a new project; instead, we'll use the existing project: `weatherweb`:

1. We add an additional HTTP request. To do this, add an additional `/temp` HTTP request by passing the `temperature_get_handler()` handler function. Then, declare `weather_temp` for our `/temp` request:

```
esp_err_t temperature_get_handler(httpd_req_t *req)
{
    ....
}

httpd_uri_t weather_temp = {
    .uri = "/temp",
    .method = HTTP_GET,
```

```
      .handler = temperature_get_handler,
      .user_ctx = "ESP32 Weather System"
};
```

2. In the `temperature_get_handler()` function, we read the temperature data from the `DHT22` module by calling the `dht_read_data()` function:

```
int16_t temperature = 0;
int16_t humidity = 0;
char tmp_buff[10];
```

```
if (dht_read_data(sensor_type, dht_gpio, &humidity, &temperature) ==
ESP_OK)
    {
        sprintf(tmp_buff, "%d",temperature/10);
    }else{
        tmp_buff[0]='\0';
    }
```

3. After doing this, we will send the temperature data to the requester:

```
httpd_resp_send(req, tmp_buff, strlen(tmp_buff));

if (httpd_req_get_hdr_value_len(req, "Host") == 0) {
    ESP_LOGI(TAG, "Request headers lost");
}
```

4. We initialize `httpd_config_t` with the default configuration, as follows:

```
httpd_handle_t start_webserver(void)
{
    httpd_handle_t server = NULL;
    httpd_config_t config = HTTPD_DEFAULT_CONFIG();
```

5. Next, we register our `/temp` request using `httpd_register_uri_handler()`. To do this, we pass the `weather_temp` variable into the `httpd_register_uri_handler()` function:

```
    // Start the httpd server
    ESP_LOGI(TAG, "Starting server on port: '%d'", config.server_port);
    if (httpd_start(&server, &config) == ESP_OK) {
        // Set URI handlers
        ESP_LOGI(TAG, "Registering URI handlers");
        httpd_register_uri_handler(server, &weather);
        httpd_register_uri_handler(server, &weather_temp);
        return server;
    }
```

Finally, we save this program.

Next, we will develop the Node.js application.

Writing a program for Node.js

In this section, we create a Node.js project. You can download and install Node.js at the following link: `https://nodejs.org`. Create a folder called `weatherfeeder.js` to create our Node.js project. Within this folder, we will create the following files:

- `App.js`: This is the main program from Node.js.
- `package.json`: This is the configuration file for the Node.js project.
- `weather.html`: This is the HTML form to display sensor data.

Figure 6.6 shows our project structure:

Figure 6.6: The project structure for weatherfeeder.js

To visualize sensor data, we can use Flot charts from `https://www.flotcharts.org/`. You can download and extract the Flot project inside our project. Let's begin by writing our program:

    1. Write scripts for `package.json`, as follows:

```
{
  "name": "weatherfeeder",
  "description": "Feeding temperature using Node.js, socket.io, and
flot.js",
  "version": "0.0.1",
  "private": true,
```

```
  "dependencies": {
    "socket.io": "latest"
  }
}
```

2. After saving these scripts, you can install all dependency libraries by typing this command in the Terminal. You should have internet access on your computer:

```
$ npm install
```

This will install `Socket.io` into your project.

3. Next, we write codes on `weather.html`. This program uses the Flot library (`https://www.flotcharts.org/`) to visualize sensor data. `Socket.io` is responsible for retrieving sensor data from ESP32. We can implement our `Socket.io` script in `weather.html`:

```
var socket = io.connect();
var items = [];
var counter = 0;

socket.on('data', function (data) {
    items.push([counter, data]);
    counter = counter + 1;
    if (items.length > 20)
        items.shift();
    $.plot($("#placeholder"), [items]);
});
```

4. Next, develop our main program in the `App.js` file. Begin by running a web server and handle the HTTP request using `http.createServer()`.

5. Then, send `weather.html` if the user requests / from a browser. `Socket.io` will serve the `data` requests on data event.

6. You should change the IP address of the ESP32 board on the `esp32_req` variable. `Socket.io` will call the ESP32 web server to retrieve the sensor data:

```
var http = require('http');
var path = require('path');
var fs = require('fs');

// change this port
var port = process.env.PORT || 80; //8345;
// ESP32 server
var esp32_req = "http://192.168.1.16/temp";
```

7. We create a server object using `createServer()` from the HTTP module. We map all paths for JavaScript and CSS files, as follows:

```
var srv = http.createServer(function (req, res) {

    var filePath = '.' + req.url;
    if (filePath == './')
        filePath = './weather.html';

    var extname = path.extname(filePath);
    var contentType = 'text/html';
    switch (extname) {
        case '.js':
            contentType = 'text/javascript';
            break;
        case '.css':
            contentType = 'text/css';
            break;
    }
```

8. We then evaluate to check the requested file. If the requested file is available, we read it and send it to the client. Otherwise, we send an error message on the HTTP header:

```
fs.exists(filePath, function(exists) {
    if (exists) {
        fs.readFile(filePath, function(error, content) {
            if (error) {
                res.writeHead(500);
                res.end();
            } else {
                res.writeHead(200, {
                    'Content-Type' : contentType
                });
                res.end(content, 'utf-8');
            }
        });
    } else {
        res.writeHead(404);
        res.end();
    }
});
```

9. Next, our server listens on a particular port using the `listen()` function:

```
gw_srv = require('socket.io').listen(srv);
srv.listen(port);
console.log('Server running at http://127.0.0.1:' + port +'/');
```

10. We listen to the `'connection'` event using `sockets.on()`. Then, we read the client request, as follows:

```
gw_srv.sockets.on('connection', function(socket) {
    var dataPusher = setInterval(function () {
        //socket.volatile.emit('data', Math.random() * 100);
        http.get(esp32_req, (resp) => {
        let data = '';
```

11. We also listen to the `'data'` event to read incoming data, and the `'end'` event to reach the end of the client data:

```
        // A chunk of data has been received.
        resp.on('data', (chunk) => {
            data += chunk;
        });
        // The whole response has been received. Print out the result.
        resp.on('end', () => {
            console.log('Received data: ',data);
            socket.volatile.emit('data', data);
            //console.log(JSON.parse(data).explanation);
        });
        }).on("error", (err) => {
        console.log("Error: " + err.message);
        });
```

12. Save the program.

Now that we've written our program using Node.js, let's move on to testing it.

Testing the program

We'll test our program using the following steps:

1. As explained in the *Writing a program for ESP32* section, compile and upload the `weatherweb` project into the ESP32 board, and then test our `/temp` request using a browser.

2. After doing this, navigate to `http://<ip address of ESP32>/temp`:

Figure 6.7: Accessing temperature data from a browser

3. You can run the `App.js` program using the following `node` command:

```
$ node App.js
```

This program will run in the background within the OS. You can stop this program by pressing the *Ctrl + C* keys.

You can see our Node.js program is running, as shown in *Figure 6.8*:

```
weatherfeeder — node App.js — 80×24
agusk$ node App.js
Server running at http://127.0.0.1:80/
```

Figure 6.8: Running the web server in Node.js

4. Now open a browser and navigate to the IP address of the Node.js application. You should see the data visualization of the temperature data, as shown in *Figure 6.9*:

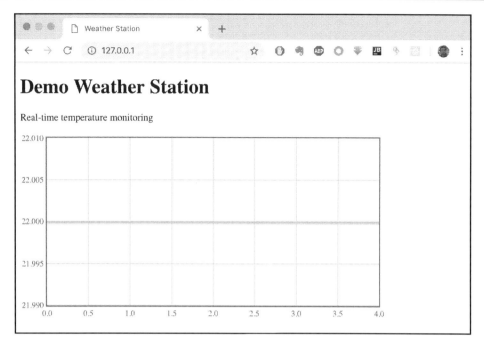

Figure 6.9: The program output of temperature data in a browser

The browser receives temperature sensor information from the `weatherfeeder` server. *Figure 6.9* shows a graphical web interface where the x axis represents the data counter, and the y axis represents the temperature value. According to the figure, the temperature value equals 22 °C.

You also can see the program output from the Node.js application, **weatherfeeder**, as shown in *Figure 6.10*:

```
[agusk$ node App.js
Server running at http://127.0.0.1:80/
Received data:   22
Received data:   22
Received data:   22
Received data:   22
Received data:   22
Received data:   22
Received data:   22
```

Figure 6.10: The server program output in the Terminal

You should now be able to see temperature data from the ESP32 board using a Terminal application, such as CoolTerm.

You can improve this project by adding additional sensor devices and new visualization models on HTML5 at `https://www.flotcharts.org/`. You can try programming samples from the Flot project.

Summary

In this chapter, we learned how to build a weather station with ESP32 and DHT22. We also extended our weather station with Node.js in order to serve massive requests.

In the next chapter, we will learn about Wi-Fi wardriving with the ESP32 board.

Making Your Own Wi-Fi Wardriving

7

Wardriving is the act of locating and possibly exploiting connections to wireless networks while driving around a certain area or region. Wardriving can be used to obtain a list of Wi-Fi SSIDs in a particular area. In this chapter, we'll learn how to implement Wi-Fi Wardriving with the ESP32 board. We can use existing Wi-Fi hotspots and maps in locations that are retrieved from GPS.

We will explore the following topics in this chapter:

- An introduction to Wi-Fi Wardriving
- Accessing your location via GPS from the ESP32 board
- Implementing Wi-Fi Wardriving using ESP32

Technical requirements

Before we begin, make sure you have the following things ready:

- A computer with an OS installed such as Windows, Linux, or macOS.
- An ESP32 development board. The recommended board here is the ESP-WROVER-KIT v4 board from Espressif.
- A Wi-Fi network with internet access.
- A GPS module.

Introducing Wi-Fi Wardriving

Wi-Fi Wardriving is the act of performing Wi-Fi hotspot profiling and then mapping the area to its current location in a certain region. Wi-Fi Wardriving is usually executed by driving with a vehicle. In this chapter, we will explore how to implement simple Wi-Fi Wardriving.

We can gather all the SSID names from existing Wi-Fi hotspots. Furthermore, we can store a result into local storage such as a microSD card. Then we can analyze the data by plotting it on a map engine such as Google Maps:

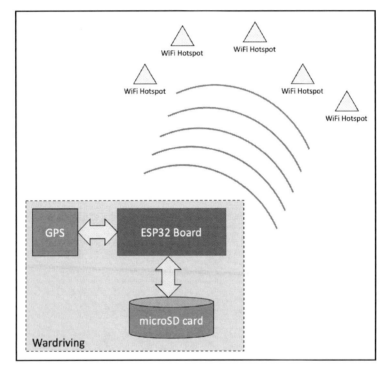

Figure 7.1: A simple Wi-Fi Wardriving implementation for ESP32

You can see that Wi-Fi hotspots are mapped onto Google Maps in Figure 7.2; these are simple fake Wi-Fi hotspot positions. You can also use other map engines to render the Wi-Fi hotspot positions:

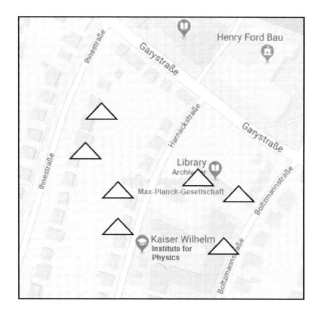

Figure 7.2: Mapping a hotspot on Google Maps

Next, we will review the GPS modules for ESP32 boards.

Reviewing the GPS module

There are some GPS modules that we can apply on the ESP32 board. The GPS module usually uses the UART interface to communicate to the board. UART is a serial communication model that can send and receive data per byte sequentially. Our board waits for incoming messages from the GPS module via UART.

The following code block is an example of the data output from a GPS module. This data shows that our GPS module cannot detect our location from the satellite. All GPS data is defined in NMEA format; further information about NMEA can be found at `http://www.nmea.org/content/nmea_standards/nmea_0183_v_410.asp`.

```
$GPGLL,,,,,,V,N*64
$GPRMC,,V,,,,,,,,,,N*53
$GPVTG,,,,,,,,,N*30
$GPGGA,,,,,,0,00,99.99,,,,,,*48
$GPGSA,A,1,,,,,,,,,,,,,99.99,99.99,99.99*30
$GPGSV,1,1,01,04,,,13*7E
$GPGLL,,,,,,V,N*64
$GPRMC,,V,,,,,,,,,,N*53
$GPVTG,,,,,,,,,N*30
```

You may not get the position of the data from the GPS module; here is a sample of GPS data with the GPGGA format:

```
$GPGGA,215322.000,5003.8239,N,12584.1234,W,1,07,1.6,1581.9,M,-20.7,M,,0000*
5F
```

For example, we can read the GPS data with the GPGGA format as follows:

- **Time**: `215322.000` is `21:53` and `22.000` seconds in **Greenwich Mean Time (GMT)**
- **Longitude**: `5003.8240,N` is latitude in *degrees.decimal minutes, north*
- **Latitude**: `12584.1234,W` is longitude in *degrees.decimal minutes, west*
- **Number:** The number of satellites seen: 07
- **Altitude**: 1,581 meters

For the GPS module, we can use SparkFun. You can find out about SparkFun GPS-RTK2 Board – ZED-F9P (Qwiic) at `https://www.sparkfun.com/products/15136.` `Figure` `7-3` `shows` `a` `form` `of` `parkFun` `GPS-RTK2` `Board:`

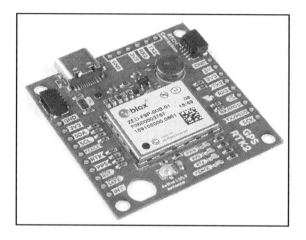

Figure 7.3: SparkFun GPS-RTK2 Board – ZED-F9P (Qwiic)

You also can find cheap GPS modules on AliExpress. I recommend using the GPS module from u-blox's modules. You can see u-blox's modules for GPS at `https://www.u-blox.com/` `en/positioning-chips-and-modules.`

Accessing your location via the GPS module

In this section, we will develop the ESP32 program to access the GPS module. For demo purposes, we use a GPS module with a UART interface. I have used the u-blox NEO-6M module. I obtained this module from DX at `https://www.dx.com/p/gps-module-w-` `ceramic-passive-antenna-for-raspberry-pi-arduino-red-2052944.`

Our demo scenario is to read UART data from the u-blox NEO-6M module; and then print it on a serial Terminal of the ESP32 board.

So, let's start!

Hardware wiring

Our ESP32 board is connected to the ESP32 board through the UART interface. The UART interface has an Rx receiver and a Tx transmitter. Technically, we can map some ESP32 GPIOs to become UART pins. In this demo, we will perform the following wiring:

- The GPS Rx pin is connected to ESP32 IOIO 22
- The GPS Tx pin is connected to ESP32 IOIO 23
- The GPS GND pin is connected to ESP32 GND
- The GPS VCC pin is connected to ESP32 3.3V

Other GPS pins are connected to the GND pin from the ESP32 board. We only use Rx and Tx from the GPS module. You can see my hardware wiring in *Figure 7.4*:

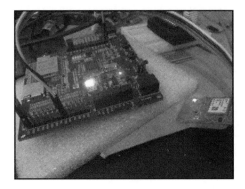

Figure 7.4: Hardware wiring for the ESP32 board and the GPS module

Writing a program

In this section, we will develop a program to read GPS data via the UART interface. Here, you can create a new project for ESP32, for instance, gpsdemo. Our main program is the gpsdemo.c file; we will implement our program in the gpsdemo.c file:

1. First, we define our header files for the required libraries in the gpsdemo project:

```
#include "freertos/FreeRTOS.h"
#include "freertos/task.h"
#include "freertos/queue.h"
#include "esp_log.h"
#include "driver/uart.h"
```

Then, we will define our UART pins for the GPS module. We also set a buffer size that will be used when reading data from the UART interface:

```
static const char *TAG = "GPS";

/* Which UART is the GPS module on? */
#define GPS_UART_NUM UART_NUM_1
#define GPS_UART_RX_PIN (22)
#define GPS_UART_TX_PIN (23)
#define GPS_UART_RTS_PIN (21)
#define GPS_UART_CTS_PIN (35)

/* Parameters for the data buffers */
#define UART_SIZE (80)
#define UART_RX_BUF_SIZE (1024)
```

In the main entry, `app_main()`, we call our `config_gps_uart()` function to initialize our UART interface.

2. Then, our program will perform looping with `while()` in order to run continuously:

```
int app_main(void)
{
    ESP_LOGI(TAG, "Configuring UART");
    config_gps_uart();

    while(true){
        vTaskDelay(3000 / portTICK_PERIOD_MS);
    }

    return 0;
}
```

3. Now we implement our function named `config_gps_uart()`. This function sets our UART pins using the `uart_set_pin()` API.
4. Then, we install the UART driver by calling the `uart_driver_install()` function.
5. After we have initialized the UART driver, we create a background task using `xTaskCreate()` by passing the `uart_event_task()` function:

```
static void config_gps_uart(void) {
    uart_config_t uart_config = {
        .baud_rate = 9600,
        .data_bits = UART_DATA_8_BITS,
        .parity = UART_PARITY_DISABLE,
```

```
        .stop_bits = UART_STOP_BITS_1,
        .flow_ctrl = UART_HW_FLOWCTRL_DISABLE
    };
    uart_param_config(GPS_UART_NUM, &uart_config);
    //Set UART pins (using UART0 default pins ie no changes.)
    uart_set_pin(GPS_UART_NUM, GPS_UART_RX_PIN, GPS_UART_TX_PIN,
GPS_UART_RTS_PIN, GPS_UART_CTS_PIN);
    //Install UART driver
    uart_driver_install(GPS_UART_NUM, UART_RX_BUF_SIZE * 2, 0, 0, NULL, 0);
    xTaskCreate(uart_event_task, "uart_event_task", 2048, NULL, 12, NULL);
}
```

The uart_event_task() function is used to listen to incoming data from the UART interface.

We implement while() to run our task continuously. Inside while(), we call the read_line() function to read the UART data ending with '\n':

```
static void uart_event_task(void *pvParameters)
{
    while (1) {
        char *line = read_line(GPS_UART_NUM);
        ESP_LOGI(TAG, "[UART DATA]: %s", line);

    }
    /* Should never get here */
    vTaskDelete(NULL);
}
```

6. Next, we implement the read_line() function. We can read UART data using uart_read_bytes() by passing our buffer characters. We read the UART data per character.

7. If we get '\n' from the UART interface, we stop to read the UART data and return to the function caller:

```
char* read_line(uart_port_t uart_controller) {

  static char line[UART_SIZE];
  char *ptr = line;
  while(1) {
    int num_read = uart_read_bytes(uart_controller, (unsigned char *)ptr,
1, portMAX_DELAY);
    if(num_read == 1) {
      // new line found, terminate the string and return
```

```
      if(*ptr == '\n') {
        ptr++;
        *ptr = '\0';
        return line;
      }
      // else move to the next char
      ptr++;
    }
  }
}
```

Then, save all the codes.

8. Next, we compile and run our project.

Running a program

Now you can compile and upload the `gpsdemo` project to the ESP32 board. To do this, you can follow these steps:

1. Open a serial tool such as the CoolTerm tool.
2. Configure CoolTerm to the ESP32 board serial.
3. Then, you can connect your tool to the ESP32 board.

Wait a few seconds so that the GPS module can get the current positions from the satellites. You can see a sample of the program output in *Figure 7.5*:

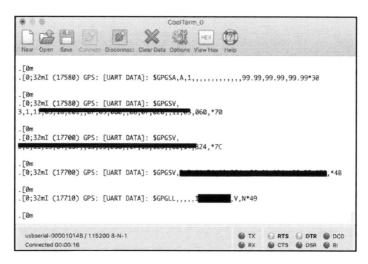

Figure 7.5: The program output from the GPS module on the ESP32 serial Terminal

Parsing GPS data

We have built the `gpsdemo` project to read GPS data via the UART interface. We can see that the GPS module output shows raw data. To obtain the current position of our location with the GPS module, we should parse our GPS data. There are a number of libraries that we can use to parse GPS data.

For our project, we can use the `minmea` library (`https://github.com/kosma/minmea`). You can download the `minmea` project and extract it into components for our project. You can see how to to implement `minmea` as the ESP32 component in Figure 7.6:

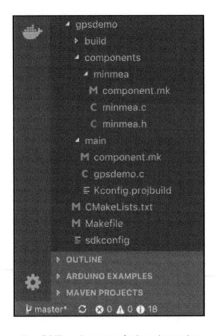

Figure 7.6: The project structure for the gpsdemo project

Now we can modify our `gpsdemo` project. We do this by adding `minmea.h` in our main program file:

```
// minmea
#include "minmea.h"
```

We also define `latitude`, `longitude`, `fix_quality`, and `satellites_tracked` as variables to hold our current GPS data:

```
// GPS variables and initial state
float latitude = -1.0;
float longitude = -1.0;
int fix_quality = -1;
int satellites_tracked = -1;
```

We define the `parse_gps_nmea()` function to parse GPS data. We can use the `minmea_sentence_id()` function from the `minmea` library to identify the GPS data type.

If the GPS data type is `MINMEA_SENTENCE_RMC`, we can extract the GPS position using the `minmea_parse_rmc()` function. We will get the `minmea_sentence_rmc` struct after calling the `minmea_parse_rmc()` function; I will identify various data types, as follows:

```
void parse_gps_nmea(char* line){
    // parse the line
    switch (minmea_sentence_id(line, false)) {
        case MINMEA_SENTENCE_RMC: {
...
                float new_longitude = minmea_tocoord(&frame.longitude);
...
            }


}
```

Our `parse_gps_nmea()` function will be called in the `uart_event_task()` function. We put this on `while()`, as shown in the following script:

```
static void uart_event_task(void *pvParameters)
{
    while (1) {
        char *line = read_line(GPS_UART_NUM);
        parse_gps_nmea(line);

    }
    /* Should never get here */
    vTaskDelete(NULL);
}
```

You can now save the codes, compile, and upload the project into the ESP32 board. Open the serial tool to see the program output; *Figure 7.7* shows my current location via the GPS module:

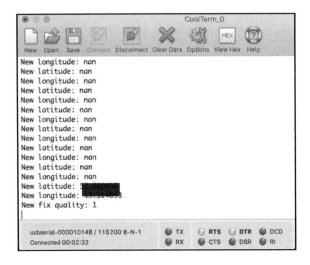

Figure 7.7: The program output from the gpsdemo project

Building your own Wi-Fi Wardriving with ESP32

In this section, we will combine our previous project with building our own Wi-Fi Wardriving with the ESP32 board – to read GPS data and the SSID name from Wi-Fi hotspots. To do this, we must read the current position via the GPS module and store it in a certain variable. Next, we perform Wi-Fi scanning to retrieve the Wi-Fi SSID.

So, let's start!

Hardware wiring

To build your own Wi-Fi Wardriving board we will use the same hardware wiring from the gpsdemo project in the previous section.

Writing a program

To write the program, we use `gpsdemo`. We add the Wi-Fi API to retrieve the SSID names on the current environment and then we start to modify the `gpsdemo.c` file:

1. First, we add the required header files to access the Wi-Fi hotspots:

```
#include "esp_wifi.h"
#include "esp_system.h"
#include "esp_event.h"
#include "esp_event_loop.h"
#include "nvs_flash.h"
```

2. Then we define the `config_wifi()` function to initialize the Wi-Fi service on the ESP32 board. We activate our Wi-Fi service as `WIFI_MODE_STA`, and start the Wi-Fi up by calling `esp_wifi_start()`.

3. We will also pass the `wifi_scan_event_handler()` function to listen to Wi-Fi events from the ESP32 Wi-FI service:

```
static void config_wifi(void) {
    tcpip_adapter_init();
    ESP_ERROR_CHECK(esp_event_loop_init(wifi_scan_event_handler, NULL));
    wifi_init_config_t cfg = WIFI_INIT_CONFIG_DEFAULT();
    ESP_ERROR_CHECK(esp_wifi_init(&cfg));
    ESP_ERROR_CHECK(esp_wifi_set_storage(WIFI_STORAGE_RAM));
    ESP_ERROR_CHECK(esp_wifi_set_mode(WIFI_MODE_STA));
    ESP_ERROR_CHECK(esp_wifi_start());
}
```

4. Now we can implement the `wifi_scan_event_handler()` function to listen to Wi-Fi events from the ESP32 Wi-Fi service.

5. When we get the `SYSTEM_EVENT_SCAN_DONE` event, we can retrieve a number of SSIDs by calling the `esp_wifi_scan_get_ap_num()` function:

```
esp_err_t wifi_scan_event_handler(void *ctx, system_event_t *event)
{
    if (event->event_id == SYSTEM_EVENT_SCAN_DONE) {
        uint16_t apCount = 0;
        esp_wifi_scan_get_ap_num(&apCount);
        printf("Wi-Fi found: %d\n",event->event_info.scan_done.number);
        if (apCount == 0) {
            return ESP_OK;
        }
```

6. Then, we get the details of each SSID data using the `esp_wifi_scan_get_ap_records()` function:

```
wifi_ap_record_t *wifi = (wifi_ap_record_t
*)malloc(sizeof(wifi_ap_record_t) * apCount);
    ESP_ERROR_CHECK(esp_wifi_scan_get_ap_records(&apCount, wifi));
```

7. We map the Wi-Fi authentication model, as follows:

```
for (int i=0; i<apCount; i++) {
    char *authmode;
    switch(wifi[i].authmode) {
        case WIFI_AUTH_OPEN:
            authmode = "NO AUTH";
            break;
        case WIFI_AUTH_WEP:
            authmode = "WEP";
            break;
        case WIFI_AUTH_WPA_PSK:
            authmode = "WPA PSK";
            break;
        case WIFI_AUTH_WPA2_PSK:
            authmode = "WPA2 PSK";
            break;
        case WIFI_AUTH_WPA_WPA2_PSK:
            authmode = "WPA/WPA2 PSK";
            break;
        default:
            authmode = "Unknown";
            break;
    }
    printf("Lat: %f Long: %f SSID: %15.15s RSSI: %4d AUTH:
%10.10s\n",latitude, longitude,
            wifi[i].ssid, wifi[i].rssi, authmode);
```

8. Next, we print all the SSID names with the current position, such as latitude and longitude:

```
printf("Lat: %f Long: %f SSID: %15.15s RSSI: %4d AUTH:
%10.10s\n",latitude, longitude,
            wifi[i].ssid, wifi[i].rssi, authmode);
```

9. In the main entry named `app_main()`, we initialize the Wi-Fi service by calling the `config_wifi()` function.

10. We perform looping to scan all Wi-Fi SSIDs using the `esp_wifi_scan_start()` function:

```
int app_main(void)
{
    ESP_LOGI(TAG, "Configuring flash");
    esp_err_t ret = nvs_flash_init();
    if (ret == ESP_ERR_NVS_NO_FREE_PAGES || ret ==
ESP_ERR_NVS_NEW_VERSION_FOUND) {
        ESP_ERROR_CHECK(nvs_flash_erase());
        ret = nvs_flash_init();
    }
    ESP_ERROR_CHECK( ret );
```

Two important aspects are now addressed. One is to configure the Wi-Fi by calling the `config_wifi()` function.

The other one is to start a separated freeRTOS task that will configure the UART for GPS connectivity and receive over the serial connection the values for `latitude` and `longitude` and those that will be paired with the Wi-Fi networks discovered in the surrounding area.

The latitude and longitude will be available in the other task by using the global variables `latitude` and `longitude`.

```
    config_wifi();

    ESP_LOGI(TAG, "Configuring UART");
    config_gps_uart();
    wifi_scan_config_t scanConf = {
        .ssid = NULL,
        .bssid = NULL,
        .channel = 0,
        .show_hidden = true
    };

    while(true){
        ESP_ERROR_CHECK(esp_wifi_scan_start(&scanConf, true));
        vTaskDelay(3000 / portTICK_PERIOD_MS);
    }

    return 0;
}
```

11. Finally, we save all the changes, and then compile and run our program.

Testing a program

You can now compile and upload the `gpsdemo` program to the ESP32 board. To do this, open the serial tool to see the program output.

Figure 7.8 shows a sample program output from the `gpsdemo` project. Here, you can see a list of Wi-Fi SSIDs with latitude and longitude information:

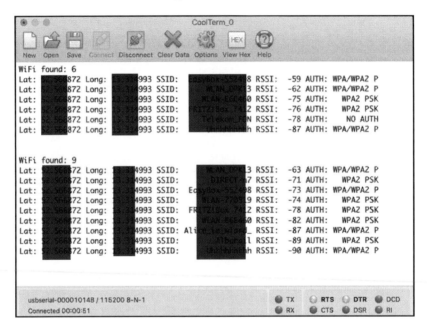

Figure 7.8: The program output for profiling Wi-Fi hotspots and GPS locations

You can also make these devices public by driving in a car or a bicycle to get more Wi-FI SSID names in the public area. When we are driving via a car or bicycle, our device performs Wi-Fi scanning to read Wi-Fi SSID names and the GPS location.

Mapping Wi-Fi hotspots to Google Maps

If we store our Wi-Fi SSIDs and GPS location in external storage such as a microSD card, we map the Wi-Fi hotspot into Google Maps. You can view Google Maps at `https://www.google.com/maps/d/`. After logging into Google Maps, you can see the web form in *Figure 7.9*:

Figure 7.9: Creating your own map with Google maps

To create a new private map, you can click on the **CREATE A NEW MAP** button; you will then see something similar to *Figure 7.10*.

Now you can upload a CVS file that consists of a Wi-Fi SSID and its locations. You should see your Wi-Fi SSID names on the map:

Figure 7.10: Uploading CVS data into Google Maps

You can experiment with what we have learned here in your own time. I recommend looking at an example of the Wardriving project at `https://wigle.net/`.

Privacy issues

Some countries may not allow you to perform Wi-Fi Wardriving due to privacy issues. You can check your local rules before you perform this task in public areas. You can also change the SSID names to random names to address these privacy issues.

Summary

In this chapter, we learned how to access the GPS module on the ESP32 board. We also built a simple Wardriving project to perform Wi-Fi profiling on a GPS location. We have read Wi-Fi SSIDs and GPS data simultaneously.

In the next chapter, we will learn how to build a Wi-Fi cam with the ESP32 board.

Building Your Own Wi-Fi Cam

8

Video surveillance is one of the monitoring systems that make it possible to obtain current information from a certain place at any time. This type of surveillance uses a camera to capture footage from a certain environment. In this chapter, we will build a simple Wi-Fi cam to take a photo with a camera and an ESP32 board.

We will be covering the following topics in this chapter:

- An introduction to Wi-Fi cams
- Reviewing a camera module for ESP32
- Developing a program for a camera and ESP32

Technical requirements

Before we begin, make sure you have the following things ready:

- A computer with an OS installed such as Windows, Linux, or macOS.
- An ESP32 development board. We recommend using the ESP-WROVER-KIT v4 board from Espressif.
- A Wi-Fi network with internet access capability.
- A camera that supports the ESP32 board.

Introducing Wi-Fi cams

A Wi-Fi cam is a system that performs sensing through a camera. With the use of a camera, we can obtain the current image within a moving video format.

In this chapter, we will focus on working with a camera on an ESP32 board. Technically, we can connect a camera module on the ESP32 board through a **Serial Peripheral Interface (SPI)** protocol. SPI is a serial communication protocol such as UART, but SPI has a synchronous interface that uses a dedicated clock signal. SPI usually has three pins: MOSI, MISO, and CS. You can find these pins on the ESP32 board layout.

The ESP-WROVER-KIT board provides a camera connector; this is shown in *Figure 8.1*:

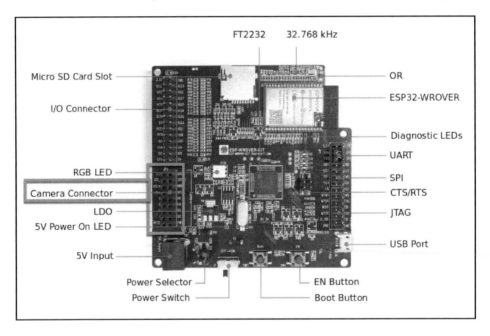

Figure 8.1: A camera connector on the ESP-WROVER-KIT v4 board

The camera connector on the ESP-WROVER-KIT board is supported by the OV7670 camera module. This module is shown in *Figure 8.2*; it is cost-friendly and you can get it at AliExpress or your local electronic store. If you use another camera module, you should create a device driver for your camera module:

Figure 8.2: The OV7670 camera module

In this chapter, we will explore the OV7670 camera module with the ESP-WROVER-KIT v4 board.

Reviewing camera modules

Technically, we can use any camera module with supported SPI or I2C protocols. One of the camera modules with this feature is the OV7670 module. This module is manufactured by OmniVision; you can find its datasheet at `http://www.electronicaestudio.com/docs/sht001.pdf`.

There are two OV7670 modules available on the market: the OV7670 module with FIFO, and the OV7670 module without FIFO. The OV7670 module with FIFO can enhance video processing.

You can identify whether the OV7670 camera module is a FIFO model or not by checking the back of the camera module. The OV7670 camera module with FIFO has an additional chip on the back of the module. *Figure 8.3* shows the OV7670 camera module without FIFO:

Figure 8.3: The back of the OV7670 camera module

Figure 8.4 shows the OV7670 camera module with FIFO. This module has an AL422B IC that uses FIFO to enhance video processing. You can use this module to get better video processing. The OV7670 camera module works with a resolution of 640 x 480:

Figure 8.4: The back of the OV7670 FIFO camera module

We can use other camera modules such as OV2640 and OV7725. These modules can work with the ESP32 board through the SPI protocol. *Figure 8.5* shows a form of the OV2640 camera module. This can work with a resolution of 1,600 x 1,200:

Figure 8.5: The OV2640 camera module

Figure 8.6 shows a form of the OV7725 camera module. This module can work with a resolution of 640 x 480 and 60 frames per second in VGA mode. You can read about the details of this camera module at `https://www.ovt.com/sensors/OV7725`:

Figure 8.6: The OV7725 camera module

We will use the OV7670 camera module without FIFO for our implementation on the ESP32 board. This camera module is cheaper than the one with the FIFO feature.

Accessing the camera from ESP32

To access the OV7670 camera module from the ESP32 board, we need to connect its pins onto the board. *Figure 8.7* shows the **Pin Mapping** recommendation to connect the OV7670 camera module to the ESP32 board:

Interface	Camera Pin	Pin Mapping for ESP-WROVER	Other ESP32 Board
SCCB Clock	SIOC	IO27	IO23
SCCB Data	SIOD	IO26	IO25
System Clock	XCLK	IO21	IO27
Vertical Sync	VSYNC	IO25	IO22
Horizontal Reference	HREF	IO23	IO26
Pixel Clock	PCLK	IO22	IO21
Pixel Data Bit 0	D2	IO4	IO35
Pixel Data Bit 1	D3	IO5	IO17
Pixel Data Bit 2	D4	IO18	IO34
Pixel Data Bit 3	D5	IO19	IO5
Pixel Data Bit 4	D6	IO36	IO39
Pixel Data Bit 5	D7	IO39	IO18
Pixel Data Bit 6	D8	IO34	IO36
Pixel Data Bit 7	D9	IO35	IO19
Camera Reset	RESET	IO2	IO15
Power Supply 3.3V	3V3	3V3	3V3
Ground	GND	GND	GND

Figure 8.7: Mapping the OV7670 camera module to the ESP32 board

One of the advantages of using the ESP-WROVER-KIT board is that you don't need an additional camera connector; you can plug the OV7670 camera module into the board.

The disadvantage of using the ESP-WROVER-KIT board is that you cannot use the OV7670 camera module with a camera connector and the LCD simultaneously, because the camera connector and the LCD pins use the same wiring on the board. You should change these pins manually if you want it to work for both the OV7670 camera module and for the LCD on the ESP-WROVER-KIT board.

Demo – building a Wi-Fi cam

In this section, we will build a simple program for a Wi-Fi cam over a network. We will use a camera module on the ESP32 board and then we will access the camera connected from a browser.

Figure 8.8 shows our demo scenario; the ESP32 board will run on a simple web server. When a browser accesses the ESP32 board, our program will send a response with a picture of the current environment:

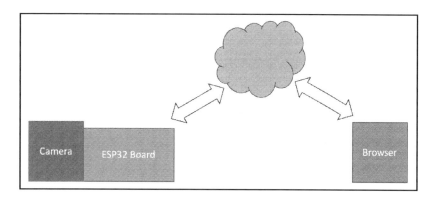

Figure 8.8: The Wi-Fi cam project scenario

For demo purposes, we will use the OV7670 camera module and the ESP-WROVER-KIT board for implementation.

Hardware wiring

If you have the OV7670 camera module and the ESP-WROVER-KIT board, you can attach the camera module into the board directly. You can see my wiring in *Figure 8.9*. Technically, our camera module and the ESP32 board are wired based on the table in *Figure 8.7*:

Figure 8.9: Attaching the OV7670 camera module into the ESP-WROVER-KIT v4 board

Next, we will develop a program to implement our project.

Writing a program

First, we create a project called `wificam`. To access the camera module from the ESP32 board, we need a camera driver. In this demo, we will use a camera driver for this project named `https://github.com/igrr/esp32-cam-demo`. This camera driver supports the OV7670 camera model.

Copy the camera and the LCD components into our `wificam` project; you can see our project structure in *Figure 8.10*:

Figure 8.10: The project structure for wificam

For project implementation, we write onto a web server and in a main program to provide the camera data from the web browsers.

Handling HTTP requests

We will now develop a simple web server to serve HTTP requests. We implement this program into the `http_server.cpp` file:

1. First, we declare our required libraries as follows:

```
#include "lwip/api.h"
#include "camera.h"
#include "bitmap.h"
#include "iot_lcd.h"
```

```
#include "app_camera.h"
#include "esp_log.h"
#include "esp_wifi.h"
#include "esp_wpa2.h"
#include "esp_system.h"
#include "nvs_flash.h"

typedef struct {
    uint8_t frame_num;
} camera_evt_t;

QueueHandle_t camera_queue = NULL;


static const char* TAG = "WIFI-CAM";

// camera code
const static char http_hdr[] = "HTTP/1.1 200 OK\r\n";
const static char http_bitmap_hdr[] = "Content-type: image\r\n\r\n";
```

2. We create a function task named `http_server_task()` to run a web server.
3. We open port 80 using `netconn_bind()`, and listen to incoming connections from the clients using `netconn_Listen()`.
4. Once our program receives a connection via `netconn_accept()`, we can process our requests by calling `http_server_netconn_serve()`.
5. Then, we close the client's connection by calling `netconn_delete()`:

```
void http_server_task(void *pvParameters)
{
    uint8_t i = 0;
    struct netconn *conn, *newconn;
    err_t err, ert;
    conn = netconn_new(NETCONN_TCP); /* creat TCP connector */
    netconn_bind(conn, NULL, 80); /* bind HTTP port */
    netconn_listen(conn); /* server listen connect */
    do {
        ESP_LOGI(TAG, "netconn_accept start :%d\n", xTaskGetTickCount());
        err = netconn_accept(conn, &newconn);
        if (err == ERR_OK) { /* new conn is coming */

            http_server_netconn_serve(newconn, queue_receive());

            ESP_LOGI(TAG, "http_server->xSemaphoreGive:::%d\n", i++);

            netconn_delete(newconn);
```

```
        }
    } while (err == ERR_OK);
    netconn_close(conn);
    netconn_delete(conn);
}
```

The `http_server_netconn_serve()` function is used to process incoming requests from the clients. In this function, we only serve the `'/bmp'` request. We send a picture that is retrieved from a camera.

We convert a raw image from a camera into the bitmap format by calling the `convert_fb32bit_line_to_bmp565()` function. To write a bitmap response to a client, we can use the `netconn_write()` function for the ESP32 API:

```
fbl = (uint32_t *) &currFbPtr[(i * camera_get_fb_width()) / 2];
convert_fb32bit_line_to_bmp565(fbl, s_line, CAMERA_PIXEL_FORMAT);
err = netconn_write(conn, s_line, camera_get_fb_width() * 2, NETCONN_COPY);
```

Then, we close a client connection by calling `netconn_close()`. We also define `unpack()` to calculate the image size:

```
inline uint8_t unpack(int byteNumber, uint32_t value)
{
    return (value >> (byteNumber * 8));
}
```

Once this is done, we save the program.

Developing the main program

Now we write our main program on the `app_main.cpp` file. First, we declare the `app_main.h` header file and store it in the `include` folder, which is present in the **main** folder, as shown in *Figure 8.10*.

The header file named `app_main.h` consists of some predefined functions that are implemented on `app_main.cpp` and `http_server.cpp`.

We declare all definitions for our main program as follows:

```
#ifndef _IOT_CAMERA_TASK_H_
#define _IOT_CAMERA_TASK_H_

#define WIFI_PASSWORD CONFIG_WIFI_PASSWORD
#define WIFI_SSID CONFIG_WIFI_SSID
```

```
#define CAMERA_PIXEL_FORMAT CAMERA_PF_RGB565
#define CAMERA_FRAME_SIZE CAMERA_FS_QVGA

#define RGB565_MASK_RED 0xF800
#define RGB565_MASK_GREEN 0x07E0
#define RGB565_MASK_BLUE 0x001F
```

We define two functions for queue processing, as follows:

```
uint8_t queue_receive();
void camera_queue_init();
```

We also declare all functions related to LCD processing, as follows:

```
void queue_send(uint8_t frame_num);
uint8_t queue_available();
void lcd_init_wifi(void);
void lcd_camera_init_complete(void);
void lcd_wifi_connect_complete(void);
void lcd_http_info(ip4_addr_t s_ip_addr);
void app_lcd_init(void);
void app_lcd_task(void *pvParameters);
void http_server_task(void *pvParameters);
#endif
```

Next, we implement our main program on the `app_main.cpp` file. First, we define all the required header files in `app_main.cpp`.

We also define the logger message as `"WIFI-CAM"`:

```
#include "lwip/api.h"
#include "camera.h"
#include "bitmap.h"
#include "iot_lcd.h"
#include "esp_event_loop.h"
#include "app_camera.h"
#include "esp_log.h"
#include "esp_wifi.h"
#include "esp_wpa2.h"
#include "esp_system.h"
#include "nvs_flash.h"
#include "tcpip_adapter.h"
#include "lwip/err.h"
#include "lwip/sockets.h"
#include "lwip/sys.h"
#include "lwip/netdb.h"
#include "lwip/dns.h"
#include "freertos/queue.h"
```

```
#include "freertos/event_groups.h"

static const char *TAG = "WIFI-CAM";

static EventGroupHandle_t wifi_event_group;
static const int CONNECTED_BIT = BIT0;
static const int WIFI_INIT_DONE_BIT = BIT1;
```

In the main entry, we start to initialize the Wi-Fi service, the camera queue buffer, and the camera device. We call `app_camera_init()` to initialize the camera device and the camera queue buffer by calling `camera_queue_init()`. To initialize the Wi-Fi service on the ESP32 board, we call the `initialize_wifi()` function:

```
extern "C" void app_main()
{
    app_camera_init();
    camera_queue_init();

    initialize_wifi();
    tcpip_adapter_ip_info_t ipconfig;
    tcpip_adapter_get_ip_info(TCPIP_ADAPTER_IF_AP, &ipconfig);
    ip4_addr_t s_ip_addr = ipconfig.ip;
```

After we have configured the Wi-Fi service, the camera device, and the camera queue buffer, we run the camera and web server tasks using the `xTaskCreatePinnedToCore()` function. For the camera task, we pass the `app_camera_task()` function into the `xTaskCreatePinnedToCore()` function. We also run the web server task with the `http_server_task()` function:

```
    ESP_LOGD(TAG, "Starting app_camera_task...");
    xTaskCreatePinnedToCore(&app_camera_task, "app_camera_task", 4096,
NULL, 3, NULL, 1);

    xEventGroupWaitBits(wifi_event_group, WIFI_INIT_DONE_BIT, true, false,
portMAX_DELAY);
    ESP_LOGD(TAG, "Starting http_server task...");
    xTaskCreatePinnedToCore(&http_server_task, "http_server_task", 4096,
NULL, 5, NULL, 1);
    ESP_LOGI(TAG, "open http://" IPSTR "/pic for single image/bitmap
image", IP2STR(&s_ip_addr));
```

The `initialize_wifi()` function is used to initialize the Wi-Fi service. In this scenario, we create a new AP SSID, called `WIFI-CAM`, by calling `esp_wifi_set_mode()` with a passing `WIFI_MODE_AP` parameter. We also set the SSID key with a value of `"123456789"`:

```
void initialize_wifi(void)
{
 tcpip_adapter_ip_info_t ip_info;
 ESP_ERROR_CHECK(nvs_flash_init());
 // set TCP range
 tcpip_adapter_init();
 tcpip_adapter_dhcps_stop(TCPIP_ADAPTER_IF_AP);
 tcpip_adapter_get_ip_info(TCPIP_ADAPTER_IF_AP, &ip_info);
 ip_info.ip.addr = inet_addr("192.168.0.1");
 ip_info.gw.addr = inet_addr("192.168.0.0");
 tcpip_adapter_set_ip_info(TCPIP_ADAPTER_IF_AP, &ip_info);
 tcpip_adapter_dhcps_start(TCPIP_ADAPTER_IF_AP);
```

Then, we activate our AP SSID using the `esp_wifi_set_config()` function. We also define our web server on the `192.168.0.1` IP address:

```
    wifi_config_t wifi_config;
    memcpy(wifi_config.ap.ssid, "WIFI-CAM", sizeof("WIFI-CAM"));
    memcpy(wifi_config.ap.password, "123456789", sizeof("123456789"));
    wifi_config.ap.ssid_len = strlen("WIFI-CAM");
    wifi_config.ap.max_connection = 1;
    wifi_config.ap.authmode = WIFI_AUTH_WPA_PSK;
    ESP_ERROR_CHECK(esp_wifi_set_config(ESP_IF_WIFI_AP, &wifi_config));
    esp_wifi_start();
```

We implement the `event_handler()` function to listen to all events from the Wi-Fi service on the ESP32 board. We listen to the following five events:

- `SYSTEM_EVENT_AP_START`
- `SYSTEM_EVENT_AP_STACONNECTED`
- `SYSTEM_EVENT_STA_START`
- `SYSTEM_EVENT_STA_GOT_IP`
- `SYSTEM_EVENT_STA_DISCONNECTED`

We connect to the Wi-Fi service when we receive the SYSTEM_EVENT_STA_START and SYSTEM_EVENT_STA_DISCONNECTED events. We then call the esp_wifi_connect() function:

```
case SYSTEM_EVENT_STA_START:
    esp_wifi_connect();
    break;
case SYSTEM_EVENT_STA_DISCONNECTED:
    esp_wifi_connect();
```

The app_camera_init() function is used to configure the camera driver including its pins. We activate our camera driver using the camera_init() function.

We map all pins to the camera module, as follows:

```
void app_camera_init()
{
    camera_model_t camera_model;
    camera_config_t config;
    config.ledc_channel = LEDC_CHANNEL_0;
    config.ledc_timer = LEDC_TIMER_0;
    config.pin_d0 = CONFIG_D0;
    config.pin_d1 = CONFIG_D1;
    config.pin_d2 = CONFIG_D2;
    config.pin_d3 = CONFIG_D3;
    config.pin_d4 = CONFIG_D4;
    config.pin_d5 = CONFIG_D5;
    config.pin_d6 = CONFIG_D6;
    config.pin_d7 = CONFIG_D7;
    config.pin_xclk = CONFIG_XCLK;
    config.pin_pclk = CONFIG_PCLK;
    config.pin_vsync = CONFIG_VSYNC;
    config.pin_href = CONFIG_HREF;
    config.pin_sscb_sda = CONFIG_SDA;
    config.pin_sscb_scl = CONFIG_SCL;
    config.pin_reset = CONFIG_RESET;
    config.xclk_freq_hz = CONFIG_XCLK_FREQ;
```

We perform a probe to test whether the camera module is attached or not. We use the camera_probe() function to do this:

```
esp_err_t err = camera_probe(&config, &camera_model);
if (err != ESP_OK) {
    ESP_LOGE(TAG, "Camera probe failed with error 0x%x", err);
    return;
}
```

If the camera module type is CAMERA_OV7670, we set the frame size of the camera as follows:

```
if (camera_model == CAMERA_OV7670) {
    ESP_LOGI(TAG, "Detected OV7670 camera");
    config.frame_size = CAMERA_FRAME_SIZE;
} else {
    ESP_LOGI(TAG, "Cant detected ov7670 camera");
}
```

Then, we initialize the camera module using the camera_init() function, as follows:

```
config.displayBuffer = (uint32_t **) currFbPtr;
config.pixel_format = CAMERA_PIXEL_FORMAT;
config.test_pattern_enabled = 0;

err = camera_init(&config);
if (err != ESP_OK) {
    ESP_LOGE(TAG, "Camera init failed with error 0x%x", err);
    return;
}
```

On the app_main() function, we run our camera task by calling the app_camera_task() function. In the app_camera_task() function, we capture the camera using camera_run(). The result of capturing the camera is sent to the camera queue buffer using the queue_send() function:

```
static void app_camera_task(void *pvParameters)
{
    while (1) {
        queue_send(camera_run() % CAMERA_CACHE_NUM);

    }
}
```

After doing this, save all the codes.

Testing

Now you can compile and upload the wificam project into the ESP32 board.

Attach the camera on the ESP32 board and set a targeted area for the camera. You can see my target area on the camera in *Figure 8.11*:

Figure 8.11: A photo from the OV7670 camera module with ESP-WROVER-KIT v4

Next, your computer should be connected to the Wi-Fi SSID name from the ESP32 board. This should show WIFI-CAM as shown in *Figure 8.12*; please connect to this SSID name:

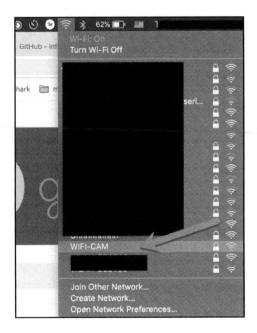

Figure 8.12: Connecting to WIFI-CAM SSID

You will be asked to enter the SSID key; type the SSID key, `123456789`, as shown in *Figure 8.13*:

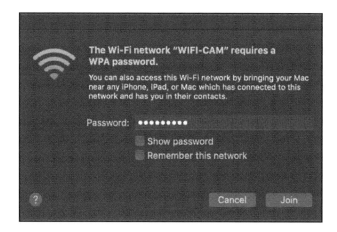

Figure 8.13: Filling the SSID key for WIFI-CAM

After your computer is connected to the **WIFI-CAM** SSID name, you can open a browser. Navigate to `http://192.168.0.1/pic`; you should get a picture of a photo captured from the camera. *Figure 8.14* is a sample of the program output on a browser:

Figure 8.14: A photo shot from ESP-WROVER-KIT v4

This is the end of the chapter. Now you can practice more with other camera models. You can extend this program for video streaming as well. In addition, you can also explore the ESP-CAM project from Espressif. This project uses the OV2640 camera module. You can visit this project at `https://github.com/espressif/esp32-camera`.

Summary

In this chapter, we learned how to work with a camera module on the ESP32 board. Here, we used the OV7670 camera module to capture the images. We also developed a Wi-Fi cam to take a picture over a network.

Next, we will explore how to use the ESP32 board to interact with a mobile application.

9
Making IoT Devices Interact with Mobile Applications

Mobile devices are now capable of performing daily tasks in the same way as a computer. People can increase their productivity with the use of mobile devices. In this chapter, we will explore how to create mobile applications and IoT devices to communicate with each other. We will use the ESP32 board as an example of an IoT device for this topic.

In this chapter, we will look at the following topics:

- Introducing a brief mobile application
- Making a mobile application and an ESP32 board interact
- Controlling an ESP32 board using a mobile application
- Using Android Studio as a development tool.

Technical requirements

Before we begin, make sure you have the following things ready:

- A computer with an OS installed such as Windows, Linux, or macOS
- An ESP32 development board; we recommend the ESP-WROVER-KIT v4 board from Espressif
- A Wi-Fi network with internet access capability
- A mobile device with Android OS
- Android Studio (available for download at `https://developer.android.com/studio`)

Introducing mobile applications

A mobile application is a common program that runs on mobile devices. This program is different from desktop and web applications due to the limited resources on mobile devices. Technically, we can develop any program on mobile devices depending on the device's capabilities. Designing UI and UX on mobile devices can also have an impact on the way the interfaces are implied.

Currently, there are two mainstream platforms in mobile application development: Android and iOS. Android is developed by Google, and iOS is developed by Apple. In this chapter, we won't focus on mobile development, but we will focus on how a mobile device can interact with an ESP32 board.

 If you are interested in Android development, you can visit the official website for Google development at `https://developer.android.com/`. You can find iOS development resources on the Apple development website at `https://developer.apple.com/`.

Making a mobile application and ESP32 interact

There are two ways to make an ESP32 board interact with a mobile application. First, we can use Wi-Fi and Bluetooth protocols to communicate between a mobile device and an ESP32 board. ESP32 has Bluetooth capability with its **Bluetooth Low Energy (BLE)** model. BLE is a version of Bluetooth technology that provides the same range with considerably lower power consumption.

If you want to make an ESP32 board interact with mobile devices, the mobile devices should have a BLE model as well. Otherwise, we cannot connect to an ESP32 board from a mobile device.

Wi-Fi is one of the most common protocols that mobile devices have. We will use Wi-Fi to facilitate the interaction of media between the mobile devices and the ESP32 board. We can use existing Wi-Fi, or our own Wi-Fi **access point (AP)**, to control a device – control will be possible just within the ESP32 Wi-Fi coverage, and having the ESP32 board in AP mode means we will not be able to control it from the internet. We can create a Wi-Fi AP on an ESP32 board, so that mobile devices can then join that particular Wi-Fi AP.

Next, we will build a project to make a mobile device interact with an ESP32 board over Wi-Fi.

Controlling ESP32 from a mobile application

In this section, we will build a project to enable an ESP32 board to work with mobile devices. We can create Wi-Fi services on an ESP32 board to allow mobile devices to perform tasks on ESP32, such as turning on a lamp and turning off a motor. Our scenario is described in *Figure 9.1*. For a mobile device platform, we use the Android application.

The way in which a smart mobile project works can be seen in the following diagram:

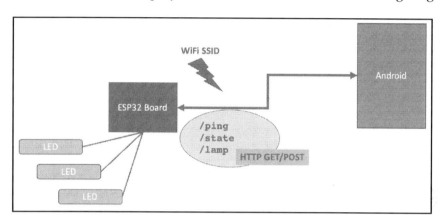

Figure 9.1: A general design for a smart mobile project

We can control three lamps with an ESP32 board through relay modules as shown in the preceding diagram. For a simple demonstration, we only use three LEDs for lamp simulation. We will expose three HTTP services: /ping, /state, and /lamp:

- The /ping HTTP request is used to perform an echo test.
- The /state HTTP request is used to obtain all the LED states that could be on or off.
- The /lamp HTTP request is used to control the LED-on or off state based on the input parameter provided by the user.

All /ping and /state request types are HTTP GET. We don't need to send parameters to perform these requests. However, a /lamp HTTP request is implemented as HTTP POST. We should specify an input parameter on the request body; we can define the following input parameters:

- Input 1 is to turn on LED 1
- Input 2 is to turn off LED 1
- Input 3 is to turn on LED 2

- Input 4 is to turn off LED 2
- Input 5 is to turn on LED 3
- Input 6 is to turn off LED 3

When ESP32 receives a /lamp HTTP request with input parameter 1, the ESP32 program will turn on LED 1. The Android application will perform HTTP requests to the ESP32 board with those request types.

Our program will run the Wi-Fi AP by naming SMART-MOBILE on the ESP32 board. Users who want to control the lamps should join the Wi-Fi SSID. For testing, I have used the ESP-WROVER-KIT v4 board as the ESP32 board sample.

Next, we will demonstrate hardware wiring.

Hardware wiring

We need three LEDs and jumper cables in order to perform our hardware wiring. You will likely need resistors if you are using a different board, for instance, 220 Ohm, to make the hardware wiring due to the I/O pin voltage level. We connect our LEDs to the IO12, IO14, and IO26 pinouts of the ESP32 board; *Figure 9.2* shows our wiring implementation:

Figure 9.2: Hardware wiring for a smart mobile project

Next, we will develop the ESP32 program.

Developing the ESP32 program

We start by creating an ESP32 project called `smartmobile` and name the main program file `smartmobile.c`. Our program will build a simple web server to serve the HTTP requests that are described in *Figure 9.1*.

Let's start working on our `smartmobile.c` file:

1. Declare all the required header files in our program. In the following code, we include the files needed to create this project:

```c
#include <esp_wifi.h>
#include <esp_event_loop.h>
#include <esp_log.h>
#include <esp_system.h>
#include <nvs_flash.h>
#include <sys/param.h>

#include "tcpip_adapter.h"
#include "lwip/err.h"
#include "lwip/sockets.h"
#include "lwip/sys.h"
#include "lwip/netdb.h"
#include "lwip/dns.h"
#include "freertos/event_groups.h"

#include <esp_http_server.h>
```

2. Define some variables with regards to the `log`, `state`, and ESP32 I/O pins. All lamps are defined as IO12, IO14, and IO26; and all lamp states are declared as the `lamp1_state`, `lamp2_state`, and `lamp3_state` variables:

```c
static const char *TAG="SMARTMOBILE";
static EventGroupHandle_t wifi_event_group;
static const int CONNECTED_BIT = BIT0;
static const int WIFI_INIT_DONE_BIT = BIT1;

#define LAMP1 12
#define LAMP2 14
#define LAMP3 26

int lamp1_state, lamp2_state, lamp3_state;
```

3. Start by creating an ESP32 project called `smartmobile`, and name the main program file `smartmobile.c`.

4. In the `app_main()` entry, initialize the **non-volatile storage (NVS)** flash by calling the `nvs_flash_init()` function. NVS is a light memory database that we can use to store key values on the ESP32 board. You can learn more about NVS in the official ESP32 documentation at `https://docs.espressif.com/projects/esp-idf/en/latest/api-reference/storage/nvs_flash.html`.

5. Initialize the ESP32 I/O by calling the `initialize_gpio()` function.

6. Run the Wi-Fi service on ESP32 with the `initialize_wifi()` function. The HTTP server handle is declared as a `server` variable; this variable is passed into the `initialize_wifi()` function:

```
void app_main()
{
    static httpd_handle_t server = NULL;
    ESP_ERROR_CHECK(nvs_flash_init());
    initialize_gpio();
    initialize_wifi(&server);

}
```

The `initialize_gpio()` function is used to initialize the ESP32 I/O.

7. Set the I/O pins as `GPIO_MODE_OUTPUT`, then set all the LEDs off by calling the `gpio_set_level()` function by passing a value of `0`. This is demonstrated in the following code:

```
static void initialize_gpio(){

    ESP_LOGI(TAG, "initialize GPIO");
    // set gpio and its direction
    gpio_pad_select_gpio(LAMP1);
    gpio_set_direction(LAMP1, GPIO_MODE_OUTPUT);

    gpio_pad_select_gpio(LAMP2);
    gpio_set_direction(LAMP2, GPIO_MODE_OUTPUT);

    gpio_pad_select_gpio(LAMP3);
    gpio_set_direction(LAMP3, GPIO_MODE_OUTPUT);

    // turn off lamps
    gpio_set_level(LAMP1, 0);
    gpio_set_level(LAMP2, 0);
    gpio_set_level(LAMP3, 0);
```

```
        lamp1_state = 0;
        lamp2_state = 0;
        lamp3_state = 0;
    }
```

8. Initialize a Wi-Fi service on ESP32 with the `initialize_wifi()` function. Furthermore, create the Wi-Fi AP with the SSID name, SMART-MOBILE, and SSID key, 123456789. Call the `esp_wifi_set_mode()` function with the `WIFI_MODE_AP` parameter.

9. Set the Wi-Fi authentication mode as `WIFI_AUTH_WPA_PSK`. To handle the Wi-Fi events, pass the `event_handler()` function to the `esp_event_loop_init()` function.

10. The following code shows the `initialize_wifi()` function implementation:

```
void initialize_wifi(void *arg)
{
    ESP_LOGI(TAG, "initialize Wi-Fi ");

    tcpip_adapter_ip_info_t ip_info;
    //ESP_ERROR_CHECK(nvs_flash_init());
    // set TCP range
    tcpip_adapter_init();
    tcpip_adapter_dhcps_stop(TCPIP_ADAPTER_IF_AP);
    tcpip_adapter_get_ip_info(TCPIP_ADAPTER_IF_AP, &ip_info);
    ip_info.ip.addr = inet_addr("192.168.0.1");
    ip_info.gw.addr = inet_addr("192.168.0.0");
    tcpip_adapter_set_ip_info(TCPIP_ADAPTER_IF_AP, &ip_info);
    tcpip_adapter_dhcps_start(TCPIP_ADAPTER_IF_AP);
    // wifi init
    wifi_event_group = xEventGroupCreate();
    ESP_ERROR_CHECK( esp_event_loop_init(event_handler, arg));
    wifi_init_config_t cfg = WIFI_INIT_CONFIG_DEFAULT();
    ESP_ERROR_CHECK( esp_wifi_init(&cfg) );
    ESP_ERROR_CHECK( esp_wifi_set_mode(WIFI_MODE_AP) );
```

In the `wifi_config` structure, we will store the Wi-Fi SSID of the AP that will be created and run by ESP8266:

```
wifi_config_t wifi_config;
memcpy(wifi_config.ap.ssid, "SMART-MOBILE", sizeof("SMART-
MOBILE"));
memcpy(wifi_config.ap.password, "123456789", sizeof("123456789"));
wifi_config.ap.ssid_len = strlen("SMART-MOBILE");
wifi_config.ap.max_connection = 1;
wifi_config.ap.authmode = WIFI_AUTH_WPA_PSK;
ESP_ERROR_CHECK(esp_wifi_set_config(ESP_IF_WIFI_AP,
```

```
    &wifi_config));
     esp_wifi_start();
    }
```

Now that the `wifi_config` structure is populated with all the information, it's time to start the Wi-Fi service by calling the `esp_wifi_start` function.

The `event_handler()` function is used to listen to all events from the Wi-Fi service on the ESP32 board. We listen to the following four events:

- SYSTEM_EVENT_AP_STACONNECTED
- SYSTEM_EVENT_STA_START
- SYSTEM_EVENT_STA_GOT_IP
- SYSTEM_EVENT_STA_DISCONNECTED

11. Start our web server by calling the `start_webserver()` function when we get an SYSTEM_EVENT_AP_STACONNECTED event from the Wi-Fi service:

```
static esp_err_t event_handler(void *ctx, system_event_t *event)
{
    httpd_handle_t *server = (httpd_handle_t *) ctx;

    switch (event->event_id) {
        ....
        case SYSTEM_EVENT_AP_STACONNECTED:
            xEventGroupSetBits(wifi_event_group, CONNECTED_BIT);
            ESP_LOGI(TAG, "sta connect");

            /* Start the web server */
            if (*server == NULL) {
                *server = start_webserver();
            }
            break;
```

12. Then, stop the web server using the `stop_webserver()` function when we call the SYSTEM_EVENT_STA_DISCONNECTED event from the Wi-Fi service:

```
switch (event->event_id) {
    ...
    case SYSTEM_EVENT_STA_DISCONNECTED:
        esp_wifi_connect();
        /* Stop the web server */
        if (*server) {
            stop_webserver(*server);
            *server = NULL;
        }
```

```
        break;
    default:
        break;
}
```

13. Use the `start_webserver()` and `stop_webserver()` functions to start and stop our web server. We can use the `httpd_start()` function to start the HTTP server, and the `httpd_stop()` function to stop the HTTP server. We should register all HTTP requests on the ESP32 board. When we start our web server, we register all HTTP requests for `/ping`, `/state`, and `/lamp` using the `httpd_register_uri_handler()` function.

    We register all HTTP requests on the ESP32 board by starting our web server, as shown in the following code:

```
httpd_handle_t start_webserver(void)
{
    httpd_handle_t server = NULL;
    httpd_config_t config = HTTPD_DEFAULT_CONFIG();

    // Start the httpd server
    ESP_LOGI(TAG, "Starting server on port: '%d'",
config.server_port);
    if (httpd_start(&server, &config) == ESP_OK) {
        // Set URI handlers
        ESP_LOGI(TAG, "Registering URI handlers");
        httpd_register_uri_handler(server, &state);
        httpd_register_uri_handler(server, &lamp_post);
        httpd_register_uri_handler(server, &ping);
        return server;
    }

    ESP_LOGI(TAG, "Error starting server!");
    return NULL;
}

void stop_webserver(httpd_handle_t server)
{
    // Stop the httpd server
    httpd_stop(server);
}
```

14. The `/ping` request is declared as a `ping` variable with `httpd_uri_t`.

15. We implement the `/ping` request on the `ping_get_handler()` function. We then send a `"pong!"` message to the requester.

We can implement the `ping_get_handler()` function, as follows:

```
esp_err_t ping_get_handler(httpd_req_t *req)
{
    const char* resp_str = (const char*) req->user_ctx;
    httpd_resp_send(req, resp_str, strlen(resp_str));

    return ESP_OK;
}

httpd_uri_t ping = {
    .uri = "/ping",
    .method = HTTP_GET,
    .handler = ping_get_handler,
    .user_ctx = "pong!"
};
```

16. The /state request is declared as a `state` variable with `httpd_uri_t`.

17. We then implement the /state request on the `state_get_handler()` function. We send all lamp states from the `lamp1_state`, `lamp2_state`, and `lamp3_state` variables, as follows:

```
esp_err_t state_get_handler(httpd_req_t *req)
{
    char buf[15];
sprintf(buf,"1:%d,2:%d,3:%d",lamp1_state,lamp2_state,lamp3_state);
    httpd_resp_send(req, buf, strlen(buf));
    return ESP_OK;
}

httpd_uri_t state = {
    .uri = "/state",
    .method = HTTP_GET,
    .handler = state_get_handler,
    .user_ctx = NULL
};
```

18. The /lamp request is declared as a `lamp` variable with `httpd_uri_t`. We implement the /lamp request on the `state_get_handler()` function. We then parse the request content and perform a task based on its content input:

```
/* An HTTP POST handler */
esp_err_t lamp_post_handler(httpd_req_t *req)
{
    char buf[100];
    int ret, remaining = req->content_len;
    while (remaining > 0) {
```

```
buf[0] = '\0';
if ((ret = httpd_req_recv(req, &buf, 1)) <= 0) {
    if (ret == HTTPD_SOCK_ERR_TIMEOUT) {
        httpd_resp_send_408(req);
    }
    return ESP_FAIL;
}
buf[ret] = '\0';
ESP_LOGI(TAG, "Recv HTTP => %s", buf);
switch(buf[0]){
    ....
}
....
}
```

The input content is from steps 1 to 6:

- 1: turn on lamp1
- 2: turn off lamp1
- 3: turn on lamp2
- 4: turn off lamp2
- 5: turn on lamp3
- 6: turn off lamp3

The following code performs these tasks to check the status of the lamps, in our case let's take step 1:

```
switch(buf[0]){
    case '1':
        ESP_LOGI(TAG, ">>> Turn on LAMP 1");
        gpio_set_level(LAMP1, 1);
        sprintf(buf,"Turn on LAMP 1");
        httpd_resp_send_chunk(req, buf, strlen(buf));
        lamp1_state = 1;
        break;
...
// End response
httpd_resp_send_chunk(req, NULL, 0);
return ESP_OK;
}
```

Then, we call the `pass lamp_post_handler()` function into the `httpd_uri_t` object:

```
httpd_uri_t lamp_post = {
    .uri = "/lamp",
    .method = HTTP_POST,
    .handler = lamp_post_handler,
    .user_ctx = NULL
};
```

Finally, save this program.

We have now seen how to to build an ESP32 program, and have checked the status of the lamps to study their states.

Next, we will develop Android application.

Developing an Android application

In this section, we will develop an Android application. You can check the system requirements for installing Android Studio on the official Android website. For the Android application, we will use Kotlin as a programming language. If you are not familiar with Kotlin, I recommend learning it through websites or books. The official Kotlin website can be found at `https://kotlinlang.org/`.

To communicate with the ESP32 board via HTTP requests, we will use the Volley library. This library can perform HTTP `GET`, `POST`, `DEL`, and `PUT` requests on the web server. For further information about the Volley library, you can visit this tutorial: `https://developer.android.com/training/volley`.

Next, we will create an Android project.

Creating an Android project

Android Studio makes it easy to create Android projects because it has good IDE functionality. We will build an Android application to access the ESP32 program in this project. Let's create an Android project using Android Studio, which can be installed for Windows, Linux, and macOS.

Once Android Studio has been installed, perform the following steps:

1. Select **Basic Activity** for the project template, as shown in *Figure 9.3*. Then, click on the **Next** button:

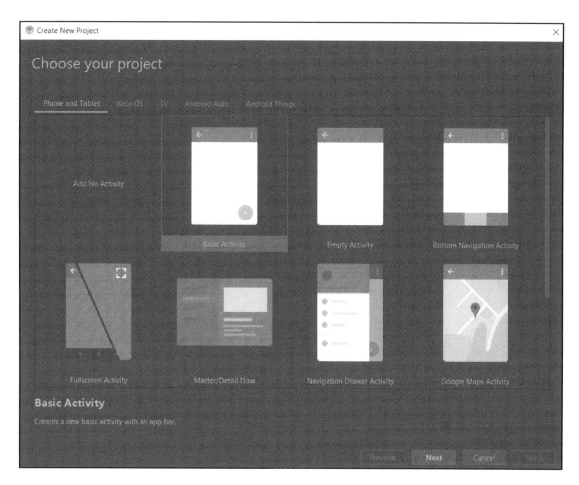

Figure 9.3: Selecting project template for Android

2. You will get a form as shown in *Figure 9.4*. Fill in your project name and select **Kotlin** as the programming language. For **Minimum API level**, you can select your own API. In this project, I used **API 22: Android 5.1 (Lollipop)**:

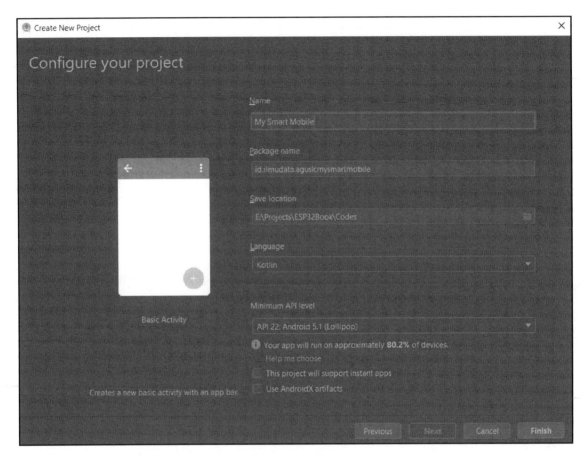

Figure 9.4: Setting the project configuration

3. After all the fields in the form's dialog box are filled in (as seen in *Figure 9.4*), we click on the **Finish** button. You will get your project files and configurations in Android Studio (refer to *Figure 9.5*).

Next, we configure our project.

Configuring the Android project

Let's start configuring the project, as follows:

1. Android Studio uses Gradle to configure an Android project. We will include the Volley library in the `build.gradle` file. You can add the Volley library by adding the following script:

```
dependencies {
    ...
    implementation 'com.android.volley:volley:1.1.1'

}
```

   Android Studio will load all libraries based on the changed Gradle configuration file.

2. Since our project accesses the internet, we should configure the security permissions by adding `android.permission.INTERNET` on the `AndroidManifest.xml` file, as follows:

```xml
<?xml version="1.0" encoding="utf-8"?>
<manifest
xmlns:android="http://schemas.android.com/apk/res/android"
        package="id.ilmudata.agusk.mysmartmobile">

    <uses-permission android:name="android.permission.INTERNET" />
    <application
            android:allowBackup="true"
            android:icon="@mipmap/ic_launcher"
            android:label="@string/app_name"
            android:roundIcon="@mipmap/ic_launcher_round"
            android:supportsRtl="true"
            android:theme="@style/AppTheme">
        ...
        </activity>
    </application>

</manifest>
```

3. Finally, save all changes in the code.

Next, we will build the UI from our application.

Building the UI Android program

We will develop a simple UI for our program; we will use two **buttons** and three **switches** to control the components.

To do this, perform the following instructions:

1. We will design our UI as shown in *Figure 9.5*. The **PING ESP32** button is used to perform the /ping request to the ESP32 board, while the **GET LAMP SATES** button is used to get lamp states from the /state request to the ESP32 board.

2. Three switch controls are represented by three lamps; if the switch control is on, we turn on a lamp:

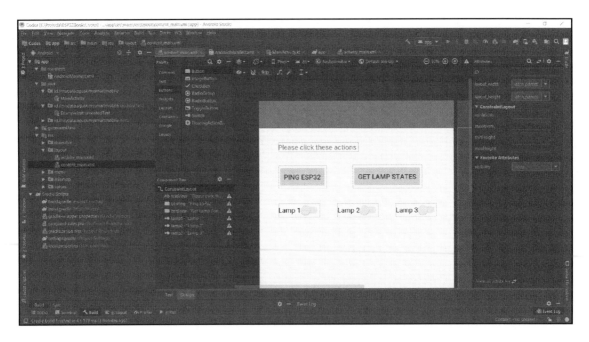

Figure 9.5: Developing the UI for the Android application

3. We implement our Android UI on the content_main.xml and activity_main.xml files. These files can be found in the Layout folder from your Android project.

4. We map our event, `android:onclick`, on all buttons in `content_main.xml`. The following scripts are the events on the button controls:

```
<Button
        android:text="Ping ESP32"
        android:layout_width="wrap_content"
        android:layout_height="wrap_content"
        android:id="@+id/btnPing" android:onClick="pingESP32"
        android:layout_marginTop="28dp"
app:layout_constraintTop_toBottomOf="@+id/textView"
        android:layout_marginStart="40dp"
app:layout_constraintStart_toStartOf="parent"/>
    <Button
        android:text="Get Lamp States"
        android:layout_width="wrap_content"
        android:layout_height="wrap_content"
        android:id="@+id/btnState"
android:layout_marginTop="76dp"
        app:layout_constraintTop_toTopOf="parent"
app:layout_constraintStart_toStartOf="parent"
        android:layout_marginStart="196dp"
android:onClick="getLampStates"/>
```

5. We also map our switch controls to changed events. We should set a control ID for each switch control. The following scripts are the switch controls on the `content_main.xml` file:

```
<Switch
        android:text="Lamp 1"
        android:layout_width="wrap_content"
        android:layout_height="wrap_content"
        android:id="@+id/lamp1"
android:layout_marginTop="156dp"
        app:layout_constraintTop_toTopOf="parent"
app:layout_constraintStart_toStartOf="parent"
        android:layout_marginStart="40dp"/>
    <Switch
        android:text="Lamp 2"
        android:layout_width="wrap_content"
        android:layout_height="wrap_content"
        android:id="@+id/lamp2"
android:layout_marginTop="156dp"
        app:layout_constraintTop_toTopOf="parent"
app:layout_constraintStart_toStartOf="parent"
        android:layout_marginStart="164dp"/>
    <Switch
        android:text="Lamp 3"
```

```
        android:layout_width="wrap_content"
        android:layout_height="wrap_content"
        android:id="@+id/lamp3"
android:layout_marginTop="156dp"
        app:layout_constraintTop_toTopOf="parent"
app:layout_constraintStart_toStartOf="parent"
        android:layout_marginStart="288dp"/>
```

6. After saving these scripts, we can move on to developing our main program.

Writing an Android program

Our main program is found in the `MainActivity.kt` file. We need to implement our control events through the button and switch controls:

1. Load all the required libraries, as follows:

```
import android.os.Bundle
import android.support.design.widget.Snackbar
import android.support.v7.app.AppCompatActivity
import android.view.Menu
import android.view.MenuItem
import android.view.View
import android.widget.Toast

import kotlinx.android.synthetic.main.activity_main.*
import android.widget.Switch
import com.android.volley.AuthFailureError
import com.android.volley.Request
import com.android.volley.Response
import com.android.volley.toolbox.StringRequest
import com.android.volley.toolbox.Volley
```

2. Define the `pingESP32()` function to receive the `onlick` event from the PING ESP32 button. Then, call the `/ping` request to the ESP32 board. A response from the ESP32 board will be displayed in the `Toast` control by calling the `makeText()` function:

```
fun pingESP32(view : View){
    val queue = Volley.newRequestQueue(this@MainActivity)
    val url = "http://192.168.0.1/ping"

    val stringRequest = StringRequest(Request.Method.GET, url,
        Response.Listener<String> { response ->
            Toast.makeText(this, "Response:
$response",Toast.LENGTH_LONG).show()
```

```
            },
            Response.ErrorListener { volleyError ->
    Toast.makeText(this,"$volleyError",Toast.LENGTH_LONG).show()
            })

        queue.add(stringRequest)
    }
```

3. To retrieve all the lamp states, define the `getLampStates()` function. This function is called when a user taps the GET LAMP STATES button. In the `getLampStates()` function program, call the `/state` request to the ESP32 board. The response result will be displayed in the Toast control, as follows:

```
fun getLampStates(view : View){
    val queue = Volley.newRequestQueue(this@MainActivity)
    val url = "http://192.168.0.1/state"

    val stringRequest = StringRequest(Request.Method.GET, url,
        Response.Listener<String> { response ->
            Toast.makeText(this,"Response:
$response",Toast.LENGTH_LONG).show()

        },
        Response.ErrorListener { volleyError ->
    Toast.makeText(this,"$volleyError",Toast.LENGTH_LONG).show()
        })

    queue.add(stringRequest)
    }
```

4. In the `onCreate` event from Android, initialize our program, including the `setOnCheckedChangeLister` mapping event from the switch controls. If the switch control value is changed, call the `applyLamp()` function to turn a lamp on or off:

```
override fun onCreate(savedInstanceState: Bundle?) {
    super.onCreate(savedInstanceState)
    setContentView(R.layout.activity_main)
    setSupportActionBar(toolbar)

    ....

    val lamp1witch = findViewById(R.id.lamp1) as Switch
    lamp1witch.setOnCheckedChangeListener { buttonView,
isChecked ->
        if(isChecked){
            //Toast.makeText(this,"Lamp 1
```

```
on",Toast.LENGTH_LONG).show()
                    applyLamp(1)
            }else{
                //Toast.makeText(this,"Lamp 1
off",Toast.LENGTH_LONG).show()
                    applyLamp(2)
            }
        }
        val lamp2witch = findViewById(R.id.lamp2) as Switch
        lamp2witch.setOnCheckedChangeListener { buttonView,
isChecked ->
            if(isChecked){
                //Toast.makeText(this,"Lamp 2
on",Toast.LENGTH_LONG).show()
                    applyLamp(3)
            }else{
                //Toast.makeText(this,"Lamp 2
off",Toast.LENGTH_LONG).show()
                    applyLamp(4)
            }
        }
```

You should write the same code for `lamp2witch` and `lamp3witch`, but change `R.id.lamp1` to `R.id.lamp2` and `R.id.lamp3`. Also, the `applyLamp(x)` function will take parameters 3 and 4 for `lamp2`, and parameters 5 and 6 for `lamp3`:

```
val lamp3witch = findViewById(R.id.lamp3) as Switch
lamp3witch.setOnCheckedChangeListener { buttonView, isChecked ->
if(isChecked){
//Toast.makeText(this,"Lamp 3 on",Toast.LENGTH_LONG).show()
applyLamp(5)
}else{
//Toast.makeText(this,"Lamp 3 off",Toast.LENGTH_LONG).show()
applyLamp(6)
}
}
}
```

5. Use the `applyLamp()` function to send the `/lamp` request to the ESP32 board. The input data is then sent to a request body. The result of the `/lamp` request will be displayed using the `Toast` control:

```
fun applyLamp(cmd: Int){
    val queue = Volley.newRequestQueue(this@MainActivity)
    val url = "http://192.168.0.1/lamp"

    val stringRequest = object: StringRequest(Request.Method.POST,
url,
        Response.Listener<String> { response ->
         Toast.makeText(this,"Response:
$response",Toast.LENGTH_LONG).show()

        },
        ....

        queue.add(stringRequest)

    }
```

Save all the codes; now you can compile the Android project by clicking on `compile` to ensure that no errors remain in the project.

Next, we perform testing for our project.

Testing a program with Postman

We will use the Postman tool to perform HTTP `GET`/`POST` testing. You can download the Postman tool at `https://www.getpostman.com/`. This tool can be used to analyze a RESTful API from a web application. We can test HTTP methods such as `GET`, `POST`, `DEL`, and `PUT` with Postman. We can also modify the HTTP header before we send a HTTP request to the server.

For our demonstration, we will first join the Wi-Fi SSID from the ESP32 program. This should show SMART-MOBILE from the SSID list; you can see this in *Figure 9.6:*

1. From our ESP32 program, we set an SSID key as 123456789. You can input the SSID key that you have entered by connecting it to the Wi-Fi:

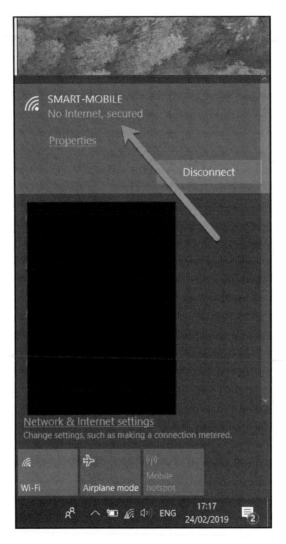

Figure 9.6: Joining SMART-MOBILE from the ESP32 SSID

2. After joining the SMART-MOBILE Wi-Fi, we can start to test our program. You can run the Postman tool for this; perform the following three test scenarios:

- Perform an echo test by setting HTTP GET with the http://192.168.0.1/ping address.
- Get all the current lamp states by setting HTTP GET with the http://192.168.0.1/state address.
- Turn a lamp on or off by setting HTTP POST with the http://192.168.0.1/lamp address. Set a request body with the 1...6 value.

3. If you have set these fields, you can click on the **Send** button to send data to the ESP32 board. You will then get a response from the ESP32 board. *Figure 9.7* shows a program output from Postman after sending the /lamp request with a value inputted as 6:

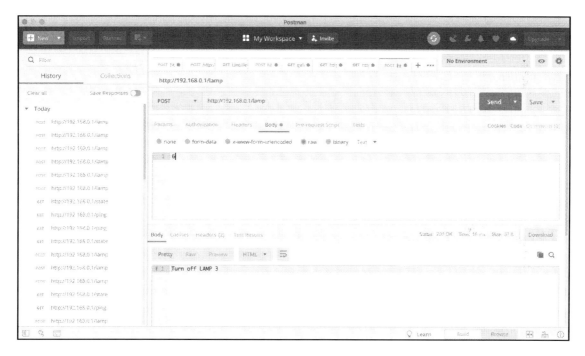

Figure 9.7: Testing the ESP32 web server with Postman

After we have successfully performed testing with Postman, we can continue to test using the Android application.

Testing the program with Android

You can test your Android application in an emulator or on a real device. In this test, I use an Android emulator. Before you run an Android emulator, your computer should be connected to the Wi-Fi SSID from the ESP32 board.

After we have deployed our project to the Android emulator, we will get our application. *Figure 9.8* shows an example of the Android application in an emulator:

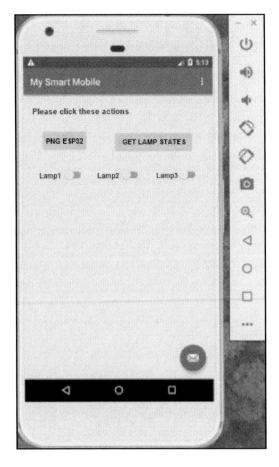

Figure 9.8: Running the Android application on an emulator

First, you can click on the **PING ESP32** button to ensure that the Android application is able to connect to the ESP32 board. If you succeed, you will see the notification as shown in *Figure 9.9*. If you don't get a response from ESP32, you should check your network on the ESP32 board:

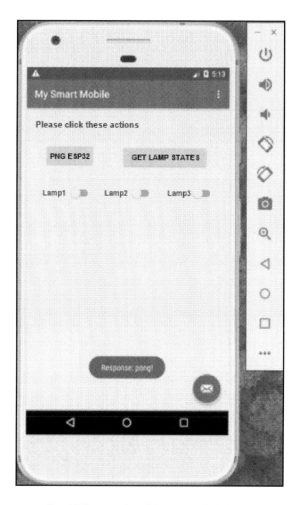

Figure 9.9: The response from clicking on the PING ESP32 button

Now you can turn lamps on or off by tapping the switch controls on the Android application. You should get a response notification from a web server on the ESP32 board. *Figure 9.10* shows a notification response when turning on **Lamp 1**:

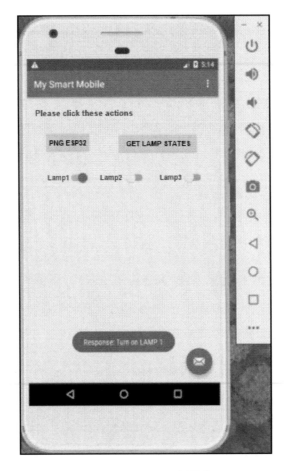

Figure 9.10: Turning on Lamp 1 (LED 1)

We can extend this project to control the sensor and actuator devices on the ESP32 board through the Android application.

Summary

In this chapter, you have learned how to develop an ESP32 program and an Android application, and then made the two interact using the Wi-Fi protocol as a communication medium. You can use this approach to control some sensor and actuator devices on the ESP32 program over the Android application. We also learned how to build a BLE service on the ESP32 board, and how to make interactions between a ESP32 board and mobile Android device possible through BLE.

In the next chapter, we will make an ESP32 board interact with a cloud system.

10
Building IoT Monitoring with Cloud Technology

Cloud computing provides advanced technology with capabilities in performance and scalability. In this chapter, we will explore how to work with cloud computing on platforms, such as **Amazon Web Services (AWS)** connect ESP32 boards. By connecting ESP32 boards with cloud servers, we can increase our **Internet of Things** IoT solutions to serve more clients.

In this chapter, we will explore the following topics:

- An introduction to cloud technology
- Connecting ESP32 to cloud platforms
- Accessing Amazon AWS and Microsoft Azure from ESP32
- Building IoT monitoring with ESP32 and AWS IoT

Technical requirements

Before we begin, make sure you have the following things ready:

- A computer with an OS installed such as Windows, Linux, or macOS.
- An ESP32 development board. We recommended the ESP-WROVER-KIT v4 board from Espressif.
- A Wi-Fi network with internet access.
- An active account for Amazon AWS.

Introducing cloud technology

Cloud technology enables us to scale our infrastructure and software capabilities. Some companies are likely to have issues with investing in software and hardware. In addition, both software and hardware need to be maintained in order to keep up performance, security, and scalability.

In general, cloud technology services provide three models that can address our business problems. The following is a list of cloud technology services:

- **Platform as a Service (PaaS)**: This service enables us to get a platform for managing applications without worrying about the infrastructure.
- **Infrastructure as a Service (IaaS)**: This service provides the infrastructure for our solution without investing in server hardware.
- **Software as a Service (SaaS)**: This service provides software that we can use any time.

Some cloud companies, such as Amazon AWS, Microsoft Azure, and Google Cloud, provide these three services. With cloud resources, we only pay for what we use.

In this chapter, we will use AWS to show how cloud technology works. Then, we will connect our ESP32 board to the cloud servers.

Connecting ESP32 to cloud platforms

Technically, cloud providers provide an SDK and API to enable access from other applications and systems. Cloud SDKs usually support some runtime and programming language in order to build a cloud application.

To connect our IoT device to a cloud server, we should check the cloud provider services for an IoT platform. Amazon AWS has a cloud service for IoT called AWS IoT. Various IoT platforms can connect and make interactions with AWS IoT. Since AWS has various cloud services, we can make our AWS IoT integrate with other AWS resources. For further information about AWS IoT, you can visit the official website at `http://aws.amazon.com/iot`.

Next, we will build an ESP32 program to access AWS IoT.

Building IoT monitoring with ESP32 and AWS

In this section, we will develop an ESP32 program to connect to Amazon AWS; we will use AWS IoT services. Our scenario is to send sensor data to AWS IoT. To perform our demo, we will complete the following steps:

- Performing hardware wiring
- Registering an IoT device
- Configuring a device security policy in AWS IoT
- Developing the ESP32 program

Next, we implement each step to build our project.

Hardware wiring

We use the DHT22 module as a sensor device for our ESP32 board. We have to use similar hardware wiring from the `dhtdemo` project, which you can read about in `Chapter 2`, *Making Visual Data and Animation on an LCD*.

Next, we should register our IoT device on AWS IoT.

Registering an IoT device

Each IoT device that wants to access AWS IoT should be registered. We will get certificate files from AWS IoT, and then we will include these files in our ESP32 board. Firstly, you should have an active AWS account in order to register an IoT device to AWS IoT.

You can follow these steps to register an IoT device to AWS IoT:

1. Open a browser and navigate to the **AWS IoT** console, found at `http:// console.aws.amazon.com/iot/home`.

2. Log in with your AWS account; if you succeed, you should see the **AWS IoT** console:

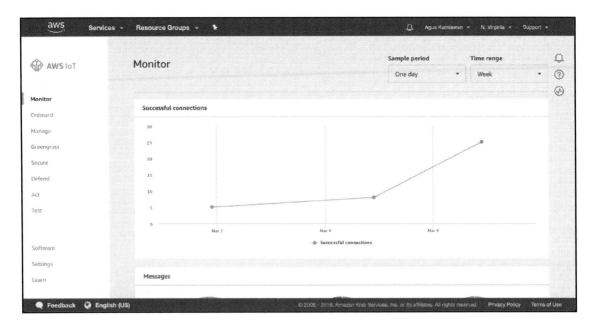

Figure 10.1: The AWS IoT console

3. Now, we create a new IoT device.
4. Click on **Manage** | **Things** in the left-hand menu.
5. Then, you will get a web form as shown in *Figure 10.2*.

6. Click on the **Create** button to create a new IoT device:

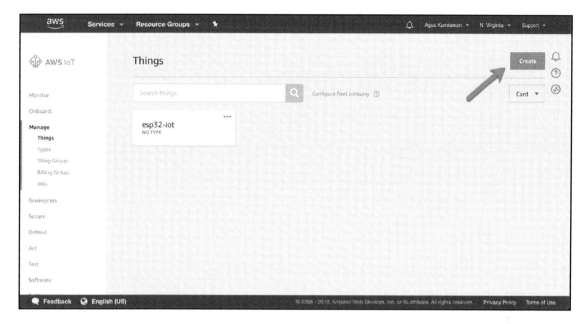

Figure 10.2: Creating a new IoT device

7. You will get a web form, as shown in *Figure 10.3*.

8. Click on the **Create a single thing** button to create a new IoT device:

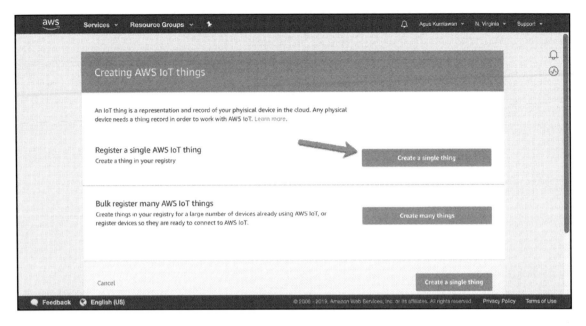

Figure 10.3: Registering a single device

9. After clicking on the **Create a single thing** button, you get a web form as shown in *Figure 10.4*.

10. Fill out your IoT device name, as shown in the following screenshot:

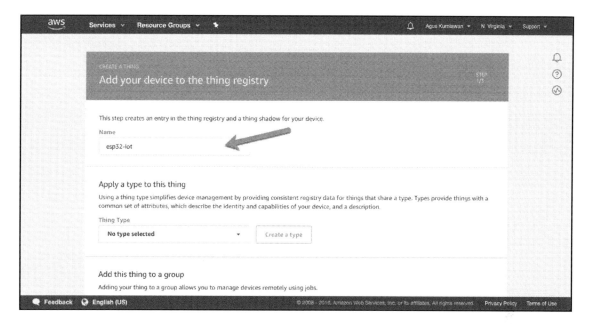

Figure 10.4: Giving your device a name

11. When this is done, we can create a certificate for our device.
12. You should get a web form as shown in *Figure 10.5*.

13. Click on the **Create certificate** button, as shown in the following screenshot:

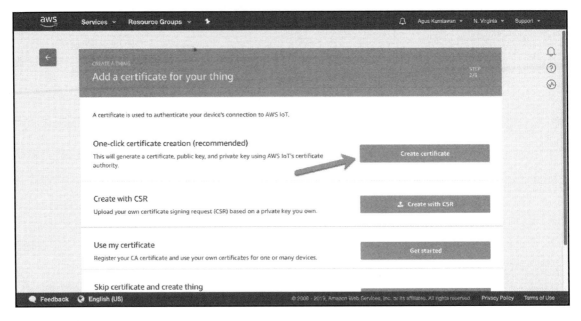

Figure 10.5: Creating a device certificate

14. After clicking on the button, you should get your device's certificates, as shown in *Figure 10.6*.

15. Download all the certificate files, including a root CA for AWS IoT.

16. After they have downloaded, you can click on the **Activate** button to activate your device and certificates:

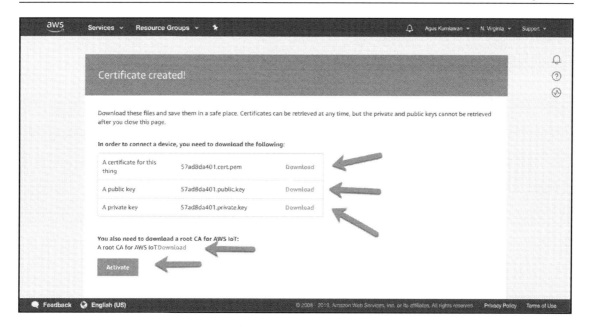

Figure 10.6: A result of generating device certificates

Now you have one IoT device on AWS IoT.

Next, we continue to configure a device security policy to enable our device to connect to the AWS IoT server.

Configuring a device security policy

Each device certificate that is created in AWS IoT should be attached with a security policy. A device security policy consists of access permissions to the AWS IoT server. If you don't attach a security policy to your device certificate, your IoT device can't access AWS IoT.

You can follow these steps to configure a device security policy:

1. Open a browser and navigate to the **AWS IoT** console, found at `http://console.aws.amazon.com/iot/home`.
2. Log on with your AWS account; if you succeed, you should see the **AWS IoT** console.

3. Click on the **Secure** | **Policies** menu so that you can get a web form, as shown in *Figure 10.7.*
4. Click on the **Create** button, as shown in the following screenshot:

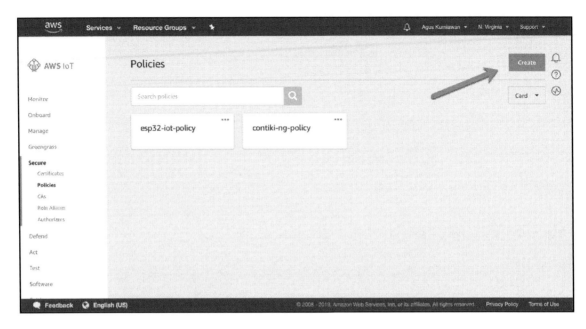

Figure 10.7: Creating a security policy

5. After you have clicked on **Create**, you will get a web form as shown in *Figure 10.8.*
6. Next, fill out your policy name.

7. Add a policy statement with the `iot:*` **Action** and the `*` **Resource ARN**. This statement enables our IoT device to access AWT IoT services:

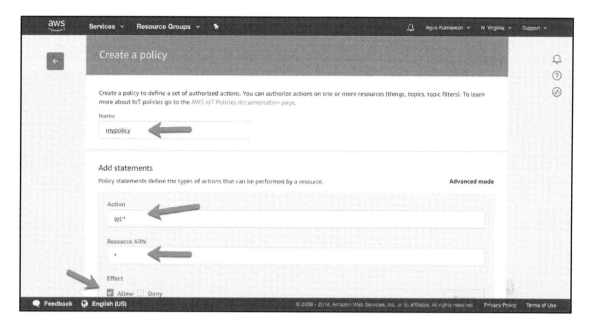

Figure 10.8: Giving the policy name and its permissions

8. Create this security policy.
9. Now you can click on the **Secure | Certificates** menu.
10. Select your device certificate and click on the **Actions** menu.

11. Click on **Attach policy** in the drop-down, as shown in *Figure 10.9*:

Figure 10.9: Attaching a security policy into a certificate

12. After clicking on the menu, you should get a dialog box as shown in *Figure 10.10*.

13. Select all of our security policies.

14. When you are done, click on the **Attach** button:

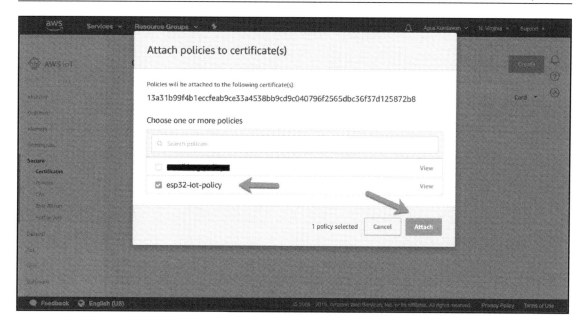

Figure 10.10. Selecting a security policy

Now your device certificate has a security policy.

Next, we will develop an ESP32 program to access AWS IoT.

Developing an ESP32 program

In this section, we will develop an ESP32 program. Our program scenario is to send sensor data to AWS IoT. We will use the DHT22 module as a sensor device; this module generates temperature and humidity sensor data. We will also learn about DHT22 so that we can focus on AWS IoT.

We will modify a project sample from Espressif. You can download this project sample at `https://github.com/espressif/esp-idf/tree/master/examples/protocols/aws_iot`.

Next, we will create a demo project.

Creating a project

We can create a project by creating a folder, called `awsiot`. You can clone the `aws_iot` project from `https://github.com/espressif/esp-idf/tree/master/examples/protocols/aws_iot`. Change the main program to `awsiot.c`, and the `Makefile` program to `awsiot`.

Our ESP32 program uses server authentication to access AWS IoT. We should put all the device certificate files into our project folder, including the root CA, the device certificate, and the private certificate.

You should put all the certificate files shown in *Figure 10.6* into the `certs` folder of the project folder. Then, rename your certificate files as follows:

- The root CA for AWS IoT is renamed as `aws-root-ca.pem`.
- The device certificate file is renamed as `certificate.pem.crt`.
- The private certificate file is renamed as `private.pem.key`.

You can see the project structure and certificate files in *Figure 10.11*:

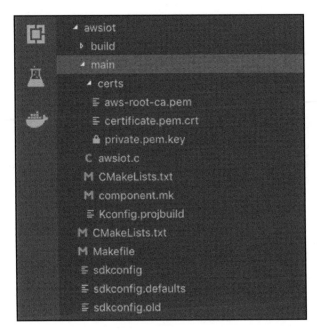

Figure 10.11: The project structure

Next, we will configure our project to enable it to work with AWS IoT.

Configuring a project

We should configure our project in order to access AWS IoT. We will configure the Wi-Fi SSID, the device certificate files, and the AWS IoT server.

You can follow these steps to configure the project:

1. Open Terminal and run `menuconfig` by typing this command:

   $ make menuconfig

2. You should get the `menuconfig` dialog.
3. Select the **Example Configuration** menu.
4. Then, you will get a dialog box as shown in *Figure 10.12*.
5. Set your SSID and its SSID key.
6. You will also need to set **AWT IoT Client ID**; you can type any ID for this value:

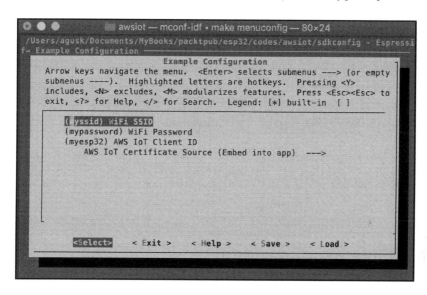

Figure 10.12: Configuring the Wi-Fi and AWS IoT Client ID

7. Once that's done, we also need to configure the certificate files.
8. You can navigate to **AWS IoT Certificate Source** to generate the certificates, as shown in *Figure 10.12*.
9. Then, you will get a form as shown in *Figure 10.13*.

10. Select the **Embed into app** option:

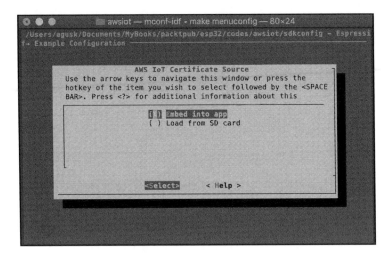

Figure 10.13: Selecting the embedded certificate files in the program

11. Now you are back to the root menu of `menuconfig`.

12. We should now set the AWS IoT server endpoint.

13. Navigate to **Component config** | **Amazon Web Service IoT Platform.**

14. You should get a form that is similar to the one shown in *Figure 10.14*:

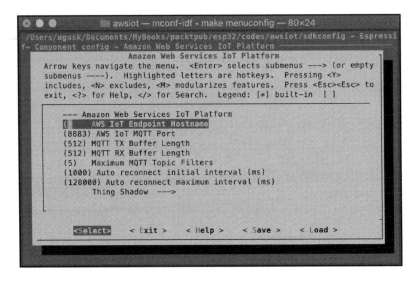

Figure 10.14: Filling the AWS IoT server endpoint

15. Select the **AWS IoT Endpoint Hostname** menu.

16. Fill out your AWS IoT endpoint.

17. You will now find your AWS IoT endpoint on the **AWS IoT** console. You will find it in the **Settings** menu, as shown in *Figure 10.15*:

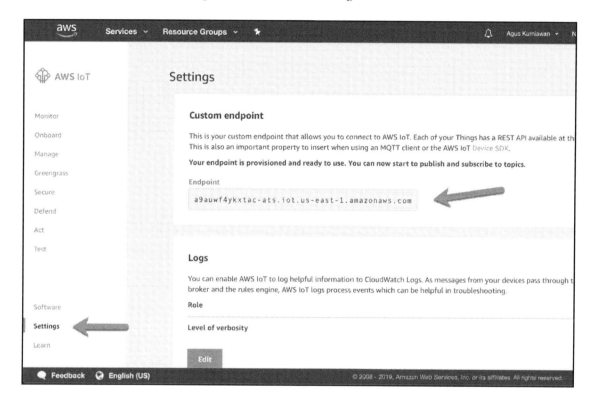

Figure 10.15: Getting the AWS IoT server endpoint name

When this is done, save all the configuration on `menuconfig`.

Next, we will write and modify our ESP32 program.

Writing the ESP32 program

To write our ESP32 program, follow these steps:

1. In the main program, using the `awsiot.c` file, we add our library header, which is DHT. We then set the ESP32 IO26 on the DHT22 pin; this is shown in the following code:

```
#include <dht.h>
static const dht_sensor_type_t sensor_type = DHT_TYPE_DHT22;
static const gpio_num_t dht_gpio = 26;
```

2. In the `aws_iot_task()` function, we need to change our AWS IoT topic to `sensor/esp32`:

```
const char *TOPIC = "sensor/esp32";
const int TOPIC_LEN = strlen(TOPIC);

sprintf(cPayload, "%s : %d ", "hello from SDK", i);
paramsQOS0.qos = QOS0;
paramsQOS0.payload = (void *) cPayload;
paramsQOS0.isRetained = 0;
```

3. We perform a looping by using a loop (such as the `while` loop used in the following code) to read the temperature and humidity data from DHT22. Then, we send this data to AWS IoT:

```
while((NETWORK_ATTEMPTING_RECONNECT == rc || NETWORK_RECONNECTED == rc ||
SUCCESS == rc)) {

        //Max time the yield function will wait for read messages
        rc = aws_iot_mqtt_yield(&client, 100);
        if(NETWORK_ATTEMPTING_RECONNECT == rc) {
            // If the client is attempting to reconnect we will skip the
rest of the loop.
            continue;
        }


    }
```

4. We use the `dht_read_data()` function to get the temperature and humidity data. To send data to AWS IoT, we can use the `aws_iot_mqtt_publish()` function:

```
    int16_t temperature = 0;
    int16_t humidity = 0;
    if (dht_read_data(sensor_type, dht_gpio, &humidity, &temperature)
== ESP_OK){
        printf("Humidity: %d%% Temp: %d^C\n", humidity / 10,
temperature / 10);
        sprintf(cPayload, "Humidity: %d%% Temp: %d^C\n", humidity / 10,
temperature / 10);
    }
    vTaskDelay(5000 / portTICK_RATE_MS);
    paramsQOS0.payloadLen = strlen(cPayload);
    rc = aws_iot_mqtt_publish(&client, TOPIC, TOPIC_LEN, &paramsQOS0);
    if (rc == MQTT_REQUEST_TIMEOUT_ERROR) {
        ESP_LOGW(TAG, "QOS1 publish ack not received.");
        rc = SUCCESS;
    }
```

5. Finally, save the program.

Next, we need to compile, flash, and test our program in ESP32.

Compiling, flashing, and testing

Now you can compile and flash the ESP32 program. Your ESP32 board should already be attached to the computer; you can type this command:

```
$ make flash
```

After the program has been flashed into the ESP32 board, you can open a serial tool such as CoolTerm. Open your ESP32 board serial; you should see the program output that shows sensor data, as shown in *Figure 10.16*:

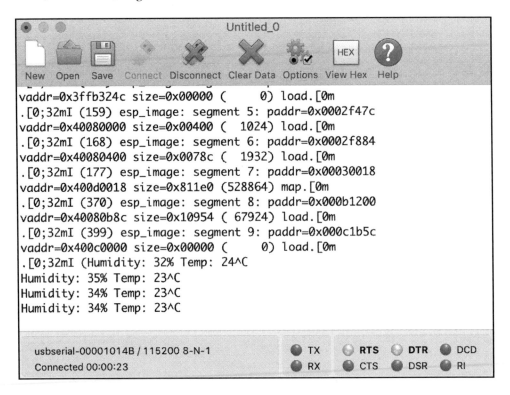

Figure 10.16: The program output on the serial tool

Now we can test our program using the **MQTT client** app from AWS. MQTT is a light protocol that is used to communicate among IoT devices. Further information about MQTT can be found at http://mqtt.org/.

Now, you can find the **MQTT client** tool on the **AWS IoT** console's **Test** menu:

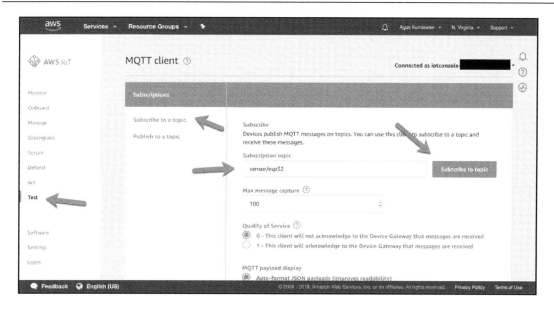

Figure 10.17: Working with the MQTT client

Set the **Subscription topic** to the topic that we have already let on our ESP32 program. Then, click on the **Subscribe to topic** button. After clicking on this, we can see the message from the ESP32 program, as shown in *Figure 10.18*:

Figure 10.18: The program output from the MQTT client

[233]

You can extend this project by adding some sensor devices to the ESP32 board.

Summary

In this chapter, we have learned how to work with AWS IoT. We created an ESP32 program to send temperature and humidity sensor data to AWS IoT. We have tried to build a communication between AWS IoT and ESP32 over MQTT. This skill can be extended to other IoT devices.

This is the end of this book. I hope you have enjoyed reading it. You can extend all the book projects for your own purpose.

Further reading

I have written a book with *Packt Publishing* about AWS IoT, called *Learning AWS IoT*. You can get this book at `https://www.packtpub.com/virtulization-and-cloud-learning-aws-iot`.

Other Books You May Enjoy

If you enjoyed this book, you may be interested in these other books by Packt:

Internet of Things for Architects
Perry Lea

ISBN: 978-1-78847-059-9

- Understand the role and scope of architecting a successful IoT deployment, from sensors to the cloud
- Scan the landscape of IoT technologies that span everything from sensors to the cloud and everything in between
- See the trade-offs in choices of protocols and communications in IoT deployments
- Build a repertoire of skills and the vernacular necessary to work in the IoT space
- Broaden your skills in multiple engineering domains necessary for the IoT architect

Internet of Things Programming Projects
Colin Dow

ISBN: 978-1-78913-480-3

- Install and set up a Raspberry Pi for IoT development
- Learn how to use a servo motor as an analog needle meter to read data
- Build a home security dashboard using an infrared motion detector
- Communicate with a web service that sends you a message when the doorbell rings
- Receive data and display it with an actuator connected to the Raspberry Pi
- Build an IoT robot car that is controlled through the internet

Leave a review - let other readers know what you think

Please share your thoughts on this book with others by leaving a review on the site that you bought it from. If you purchased the book from Amazon, please leave us an honest review on this book's Amazon page. This is vital so that other potential readers can see and use your unbiased opinion to make purchasing decisions, we can understand what our customers think about our products, and our authors can see your feedback on the title that they have worked with Packt to create. It will only take a few minutes of your time, but is valuable to other potential customers, our authors, and Packt. Thank you!

Index

20760792R00145

Printed in Great Britain
by Amazon